Suddenly, a shot rang out behind us. A VC hidden in a cluster of dense vegetation near the culvert was firing at the command group. . . . Kaylor, an expert with the M16, spotted the concealed VC first and fired into the undergrowth to our right rear. Top followed up with a shotgun blast, while I fired a burst from my CAR15. The dead VC, riddled with bullet holes, rolled out of the brush.

I glanced to my right to see if Charlie and Alpha were still on line. The mech infantry grunts were already on the edge of the cemetery, pushing on almost too quickly. . . .

I glanced across the road and saw that the mech infantry troopers had swept past some concealed enemy positions. Suddenly, I saw a VC stand up in a spider hole and shoot an Alpha Company trooper in the back of the head. The trooper lurched forward, dead before he hit the ground. The soldier had just walked past the position; he never saw it. Kaylor saw what happened the same time I did, and in a flash of a second he squeezed off a three-round burst at the VC. His rounds found their mark, and the VC's head exploded. The VC's comrades returned Kaylor's fire from a nearby dugout position. We were pinned down. . . .

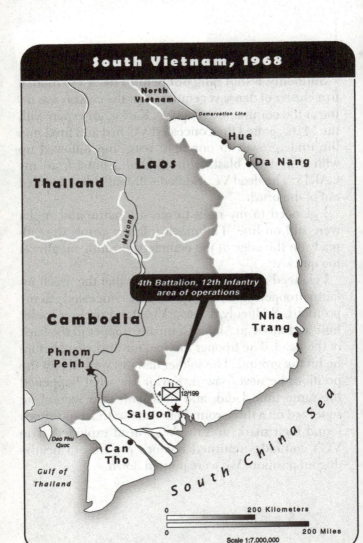

South Vietnam, 1968

North Vietnam

Demarcation Line

Hue

Da Nang

Laos

Thailand

Mekong

4th Battalion, 12th Infantry area of operations

Cambodia

Nha Trang

Phnom Penh

Saigon

4 12/199

Dao Phu Quoc

Can Tho

Gulf of Thailand

South China Sea

0   200 Kilometers

0   200 Miles

Scale 1:7,000,000

contents

For the brave Warriors of the 4th Battalion, 12th Infantry, who gave their lives for their country, and for the men who shared their foxholes during 1968.

frightening and bewildering. Over time, the ripple effects of these upheavals spread to the troops serving in Vietnam and added to their burdens.

The people, dates, locations, and operations described in this book are real and documented in official Army records at the National Archives and Records Administration. These records include battalion, brigade, and II Field Force after-action reports, brigade and battalion special orders, and battalion daily staff journals. Personal recollections are supported by numerous personal letters written by the author during the period covered in this book. Finally, many of the episodes described are based on discussions and input from other members of Charlie Company.

Keep in mind that descriptions of events in this book are from my perspective as an officer and company commander, or a "lifer," as the grunts described their officers and senior noncommissioned officers. Frontline officers and their troops shared many of the same hardships, but without question the officers, most of whom spent only six months of their twelve-month tour in a rifle company, suffered less physical hardship. On the other hand, one can argue that the lieutenants and captains of rifle companies endured more mental anguish than their men; making life-and-death decisions in combat is a terrible responsibility.

Today, Americans wrestle with the concept of heroism. Plenty of heroes are in this story. They are the grunts, riflemen, machine gunners, M79 grenadiers, and mortar crewmen. They were tough, dirty, and often profane but loveable characters who fought much more for each other than for the cause in Vietnam. The grunts of Charlie Company are the real heroes of this story.

Robert Tonsetic
March 2002

preface

This book is essentially a personal history of my experiences as a rifle company commander in the 4th Battalion, 12th Infantry, U.S. Army, during the first six months of 1968, the bloodiest year of the Vietnam War. The heaviest fighting occurred during the enemy's January and February Tet Offensive and the May Offensive of that year.

In the time between these enemy offensives, the 4/12th Infantry, known as the Warriors, participated in several large-scale search-and-destroy operations in the III Corps area. During these jungle operations, short-but-deadly firefights with Vietcong (VC) and North Vietnamese Army (NVA) units often interrupted the tedium. Charlie Company of the Warrior battalion was no different from hundreds of other rifle companies that fought during this period. Some outfits undoubtedly saw as much or more fighting than did Charlie Company, and this book's intent is not to gain Charlie Company any special acclaim, but to provide an account of the events experienced by a typical U.S. Army rifle company in Vietnam.

The events of 1968, both in Vietnam and on the home front, were tumultuous; few other years in American history can compare. From the perspective of the American soldier serving in Vietnam, the events at home were both that appear in the book. A special thanks is also due the author's sister, Joan Tonsetic, who had the foresight to save and preserve the letters that I wrote during my Vietnam service.

I am also most grateful to Thomas Fairfull, Staff Historian Headquarters Pacific Command and former director of the 82d Airborne Museum and U.S. Army Museum Hawaii; Cliff Kaylor, readjustment counselor, Eugene, Oregon Vet Center; and Lt. Mark Tonsetic, U.S. Navy, for reading the manuscript and offering suggestions for improvement before it was submitted for publication. In addition, I would like to thank Keith William Nolan, acclaimed author of ten books on the Vietnam War, for encouraging me to write the book and suggesting a publisher. My sincere appreciation is also extended to distinguished military historian and author Eric Hammel, who, as editor, guided me through the publication process with patience and understanding.

Last but not least, I offer my gratitude and thanks to my wife, Polly Tonsetic, and sons Michael and Mark for their love, understanding, and support during the many months that it took to research and write this book.

acknowledgments

The author thanks the many Warrior battalion and 199th Light Infantry Brigade veterans who over the past ten years shared their recollections and memories of the events described in *Warriors*. In particular, I appreciate the insight and contributions made by 1st Sgt. George Holmes (retired), RTOs Cliff Kaylor and Bob Archibald, Col. Paul Viola (retired), Maj. Paul Lange (retired), Michael Hinkley, Nick Snyder, Michael Raugh, and Russ Vibberts, who served in the 2/47th Infantry, 9th Infantry Division. I am also most grateful to Major Generals Robert Forbes and Frederick Davison who, before they passed, encouraged me to write about Vietnam experiences.

Additionally, the author thanks and commends the efforts of Bob Stanard and Larry McDougal, historians of the 199th Light Infantry Brigade Association, who compiled and shared a number of brigade after-action reports, summaries, and maps used in my research. Clifford Snyder, military archivist at the National Archives, was also extremely helpful in identifying and locating after-action reports, unit orders, and daily staff journals of the Warrior battalion. Also, I would like to thank Mike Podolny of MP Cartographics for his work in preparing the maps for *Warriors*, and Mike Swearingen for preserving many of the photographs

chapter one

programmed for war

As if I were a river
The harsh age changed my course
Replaced one life with another...
—ANNA AKHMATOVA,
"As if I Were a River"

October 1967, Bien Hoa, Vietnam

I awoke as the giant transport aircraft lurched into a steep final descent. As we broke through the cloud cover, the pilot centered the nose of the aircraft on the pattern of blue lights marking the runway before he lowered the landing gear. Seconds after a jarring touchdown, the four jet engines of the C-141 transport screamed into reverse thrust. The soldiers on board braced themselves as best they could in the nylon paratrooper seats as the giant transport barreled down the dark nine-thousand-foot runway of Bien Hoa Air Base. The decelerating aircraft turned abruptly onto a right taxiway and lumbered slowly toward a group of cinder-block buildings some five hundred meters away. Day 1 of my 365-day tour in the Republic of South Vietnam began.

Inside the aircraft, the temperature and humidity soared as the air-conditioning shut down. The cramped soldiers jostled and cursed each other as they scrambled to find their gear. Most of the men had napped fitfully on the final leg of the flight from the refueling stop at Yokota, Japan. A few had slept deeply as if anesthetized by the steady whine of the jet engines. Others who had dozed with their limbs outstretched made movement to and from the latrine at the nose of the aircraft difficult. The C-141 was decidedly less comfortable than the chartered commercial flights that transported the majority of soldiers to Vietnam.

The rear hydraulic cargo ramp of the aircraft lowered to the tarmac, and a mixture of dank tropical air and jet exhaust fumes flooded the passenger compartment. A helmeted military policeman in a sweat-soaked flak jacket dismounted his jeep behind the aircraft and walked quickly toward me. As senior Army officer on board, I was the designated aircraft troop commander.

"Captain, move these troops on the double to those buses beside the terminal building. No smoking on this ramp or on the buses. You've got ten minutes to get them loaded up."

"Where the hell are we going, Sergeant?" I blurted out at the MP.

"The 90th Replacement Battalion," the MP barked over his shoulder. "Now, get them grunts loaded up, Sir!"

Thus began my first mission in Vietnam.

I arrived in Vietnam better trained for this war than most. My first real-life and work experience out of school was the Army. With a degree in English literature and no transferable knowledge or skills of use to the Army, such as building a road or a bridge, developing and operating a communications network, or supervising a clerical staff, was commissioned as a second lieutenant of infantry.

At age twenty-five, with three years of infantry and Special Forces training behind me, I had acquired a credible level of expertise in the art of war. I could accurately fire, assemble and disassemble an array of small arms—everything from an M16 rifle to a .50-caliber machine gun. I had mastered the deadly skills of adjusting mortar and artillery fire, blowing up a bridge with plastic explosives, directing an air strike, leading an attack on an enemy-held position, and parachuting behind enemy lines on a night raid. I had practiced these skills for two years on numerous field-training exercises, first as a student at Fort Benning, then as a platoon leader at Fort Hood, and later as a Special Forces officer at Fort Bragg.

A one-year assignment in Thailand with Special Forces served as a practicum, during which I was able to hone my skills in the rice paddies and jungles. I also read every counterinsurgency manual and book on guerrilla warfare that I could lay my hands on. Before departing Thailand for Vietnam, the Army sent me to the British Jungle Warfare School in Malaysia for a six-week course in jungle operations—my final dress rehearsal for war.

The British cadres at the school were all experts in jungle warfare, having battled Chinese terrorists during the Malaya Emergency, and later, Indonesian troops in Borneo. A number of the instructors had served in the Parachute and Special Air Service (SAS) and regiments.

The final exam for the course was a two-week patrol in the dense jungles of Malaysia, tracking and being tracked by elite and fearsome Gurkha troops who played the role of the enemy guerrillas. We learned and relearned the techniques of ambushes and counterambushes, land navigation, river crossings, and night operations. This six weeks of training would serve me well in the months ahead.

My confidence and youthful optimism were at an all-time high. I had no comprehension and little interest in learning the politics behind this war. Nor could I even imagine the horrific long-term consequences of combat on the human mind and spirit. As a twenty-five-year-old, I didn't contemplate for long the possibility of my own premature death. I viewed Vietnam as a great adventure in which my military skills and manhood would be tested.

In retrospect, I believe that my generation was programmed for war during our most impressionable years.

My earliest childhood recollections are related to World War II. During the war, our family lived in Defense Worker Housing across the Monongahela River from the Homestead Steelworks in Pittsburgh, where my father worked. I was too young to comprehend fully the events of that war, but I do have recollections of practice air raid blackouts, ration stamps stored in a kitchen drawer, a ball of tinfoil that I saved for the war effort, and a leather aviator jacket that was a birthday gift from my grandfather. I also remember my mother's tears when my father finally received his draft notice a few days before V-J Day. He never had to go.

Several months after the war ended, my uncle returned from the Army after serving three hellish years in the jungles of New Guinea. After giving me a set of his cloth sergeant's chevrons and his overseas cap, he asked my mother to burn all his uniforms.

All of the boys in our neighborhood played war in the nearby woods. Toy rifles, Army canteens, and pistol belts donated by fathers and uncles were highly prized. We defended our woods against hordes of imaginary Japanese and German soldiers, overcoming impossible odds and accomplishing extraordinary feats of valor.

It is impossible to estimate the effect the war had on our young minds. During the war and postwar years, it was all that adults talked about and all that we saw in Saturday matinee movies and newsreels. Films like *Back to Bataan*, *Sands of Iwo Jima*, and *Flying Leathernecks* left strong impressions on our young minds. At age six, we dreamed and fantasized of the day when we would take up arms and defend our country's honor in some remote tropical jungle, returning home with a chest full of medals. These dreams of becoming a warrior were indelibly etched on my psyche at a very young age.

The war had a direct impact on my family's future. The Steelworker's Union negotiated with U.S. Steel to compensate its workers for overtime worked during the war. My father received enough compensation to make a down payment on a modest five-room house. Our family became a part of the great postwar migration to the suburbs brought on by an acute housing shortage in the cities. We moved to Penn Township, a sprawling suburban community nestled in the hills some fifteen miles east of the city.

In contrast to the decaying mill towns, everything was new and clean in the twenty-four-square-mile suburb. We moved into a tract housing development of some 750 single-unit homes. The brick five- and six-room cookie-cutter houses were small but comfortable. Transported by a shiny new yellow school bus, I attended a new elementary school with greenboards instead of blackboards. My family shopped at a new A&P supermarket stocked full of canned goods and frozen TV dinners. On Saturdays we drove several miles to shop at the Miracle Mile, one of the country's first shopping malls, and on Sunday we attended Mass at the new Saint Bartholomew's Catholic church. The contours of new lawns and clean streets delivered the unspoken message that the neighborhood was a safe and secure place to grow up.

My adolescent years were fairly typical for the 1950s. I had a paper route, and I joined the football team in ninth grade. I was too small to make the varsity team, so I switched to track and cross country in high school, lettering in both sports. Summers were an endless succession of hazy warm days and Little League baseball games interrupted only by a one-week family vacation at the Jersey shore. At fifteen, I was old enough to caddy at the golf course; this relieved some of the boredom of growing up in suburbia and provided an earning opportunity.

Memories of my younger years receded. The Korean War, called a police action back then, was remote and had no impact on my family. I gave no serious thought to future military service during the 1950s. Nevertheless, the Cold

War did have an unforeseen impact on my future education.

The launch of Sputnik in 1957 was a shock to all of us. It appeared that the Soviets were outpacing us in the classroom, particularly in science and math. They were graduating better engineers and scientists—or so we were led to believe. The push was on to close the gap. Guidance counselors began to steer brighter students toward careers in the science and engineering professions. All of this was not lost on my parents, who encouraged me to pursue a university education.

After I graduated from high school in 1960, I was accepted at the University of Pittsburgh, where I would pursue a degree in electrical engineering. This fit my parents' plan for my future: a well-paying job with a local employer such as Westinghouse, marrying a good Catholic girl, and raising a family. My family struggled to meet tuition costs at Pitt even though I had won a partial scholarship. With four other children to raise, my parents were unable to afford the expense of my living on campus, so I lived at home. Many of my freshman classmates were also commuter students from similar blue-collar working-class families. Most came from the mill towns up and down the Allegheny and Monongahela river valleys—towns like McKeesport, Clairton, Aliquippa, and Hazelwood.

Attending college while still living under the direct supervision of my parents was disappointing. Like most eighteen-year-olds, I yearned to be independent from my parents and the confines of our suburban community. I probably would have dropped out of Pitt after my first semester had it not been for my parents' dream of having their only son graduate from college. Although I passed all my courses, I hated the engineering classes, which I found to be particularly dull. Consequently, I transferred out of the engineering college to find a place for myself in the liberal arts.

I was unable to find a summer job between my freshman and sophomore years, so I enrolled for the summer term. I also enrolled in the ROTC that summer. The year was 1961, three years before the incident in the Gulf of Tonkin; no one foresaw the commitment of U.S. troops in Vietnam. Nevertheless, there was still the peacetime draft, and I thought that serving my two years as an officer would be better than being drafted and entering the service as a private.

Little political dissent existed among the students at Pitt during my university years. This was the Kennedy era. The only open expression of student unrest occurred during the Cuban Missile Crisis of 1962, when a small group of student activists held a pro-Castro demonstration in front of the student union. A spontaneous counter-demonstration by more than two hundred students soon dispersed the fewer than twenty protestors. Students who expressed a veritable hatred for the country that had nurtured them perplexed most of us.

I graduated from the University of Pittsburgh in the spring of 1964 and reported for duty as a newly commissioned infantry second lieutenant during the summer of that year. Less than a year later, on 6 March 1965, the first two battalions of U.S. Marines went ashore in Vietnam, followed two months later by the Army's 173d Airborne Brigade. At that time I was serving as a platoon leader in a mechanized infantry battalion at Fort Hood, Texas. Our designated wartime mission was to reinforce U.S. forces in Germany, and this is what we trained for until the summer of 1965, when the training emphasis began to shift. Counterinsurgency training suddenly came to the forefront.

We were ordered to put most of our armored personnel carriers into administrative storage and begin dismounted infantry training. Several officers in my battalion received orders for Vietnam, and I thought it was just a matter of time before my name appeared on a levy.

Because few Army officers had Vietnam experience at this time, the Army sent a Special Forces team to Fort Hood to instruct us in counterguerrilla operations. The Green Beret team members all had served in Vietnam on six-month temporary duty tours and knew their business well. I was so impressed by their stories and specialized skills that I immediately volunteered for Special Forces training. If I had to go to war, I wanted to go as a Green Beret.

The three-month Special Forces officer's course met all my expectations. I graduated in the spring of 1966, fully expecting orders to the 5th Special Forces Group in Vietnam. Instead I was assigned, along with several of my classmates, to a Special Forces company at Fort Bragg. The company was preparing for deployment to Thailand.

Communist insurgents were becoming a threat in the northeastern and southern provinces of Thailand, and our mission was to provide counterguerrilla training to the Royal Thai Army. When we learned that we were barred from any direct fighting with the insurgents, we were disappointed. Instead, we would be fighting by proxy as instructors. We established three up-country camps and put Thai army units through grueling monthlong counterguerrilla training exercises in the jungles and rice paddies surrounding the camps.

I was initially assigned to the training camp in the south, a few miles from the Malaysian border, where several elusive guerrilla bands operated. Later I served as an infantry training officer with a Thai regiment preparing to deploy to Vietnam. By the end of my tour I was quite familiar with jungle operations and was confident that my Thai experience would be useful in Vietnam.

At the end of my twelve-month assignment in Thailand, I opted for an intratheater transfer to Vietnam. As a newly promoted infantry captain, I wanted the opportunity to command an infantry company, so I specifically requested assignment to an infantry division or brigade. The Army granted my request and issued orders for me to report to the 199th Light Infantry Brigade in the Republic of South Vietnam. After a thirty-day leave in the States, I reported to Travis Air Force Base, California, for my flight to Vietnam.

The men hefted their overloaded duffel bags onto a baggage truck and boarded the olive drab Army buses. A second MP jeep with a pedestal-mounted M60 machine gun rolled into position at the rear of the buses as the sergeant's jeep took the lead position in the small convoy. Five minutes later, the convoy moved out toward the main gate of the air base. After passing a sandbagged guard post, the vehicles drove off into the darkness. The convoy moved rapidly along the darkened streets. On the edge of the city, we passed a crowded slum of dilapidated plywood shacks and shanties. The air was warm and heavy with putrid odors of rotting garbage, fish, burning charcoal, and cooking oil. The streets were deserted, but I saw a few eyes peering at us from the darkened doorways.

The vehicles passed through a rubber plantation that separated the city of Bien Hoa from the sprawling U.S. Army base at Long Binh, some three miles to the east. The headlights of the jeeps and buses in the convoy were dimmed to blackout drive as the vehicles negotiated the shadowy highway.

As they peered through the moonlit rows of rubber trees that bordered the road, the men fell silent, sensing the danger of this part of their journey. Except for the MPs, none of us was armed. We would not be issued weapons until we joined our units.

The convoy rounded a curve, and the landscape changed again, now to an open expanse of countryside. In the moonlight, we could see a broad panorama of rice paddies broken by intersecting lines of paddy dikes and palm groves.

Far off, a stream of red tracer rounds from an automatic

weapon arched out over the horizon toward a faraway tree line, too distant to cause any alarm. Overhead, an illumination flare oscillated downward to the earth; its unnatural glare cast stark shadows across the landscape.

The convoy reached a road junction, turned south, and rolled on past a large military compound protected by barbed-wire fences and rolls of concertina wire. Sandbagged bunkers and observation towers dotted the perimeter. Row after row of olive drab tents stood behind the wire. Closer to the highway a dozen or more helicopters sat behind sandbag revetments adjacent to a helipad. After a few more miles, the lead MP jeep wheeled sharply to the left and entered the gate of the 90th Replacement Battalion.

Two sergeants met the buses. One took charge of the enlisted soldiers, marching them off toward a distant row of tents. The other sergeant directed me and four lieutenants to the officer billets.

"Find a cot in one of the first three tents. Latrines are down the hill past the last tent; otherwise, you can stay in your racks until morning." The sergeant added one further gratuitous piece of advice: "Don't go wandering around the area in the dark or one of those FNG guards might blow your heads off."

Entering the first tent, I dropped my duffel on the wooden floor and collapsed onto the soiled, mildewed cot. The temperature inside the tent was stifling and the air reeked of sweat, canvas, and mildew. As raindrops began to pelt the taut canvas above my head, a dark, dreamless sleep engulfed me.

chapter two
the light brigade

Viva la New Brigade!
Viva la Old One, too!
—THOMAS DAVIS,
"Clare's Dragoons"

After a half-day of filling out forms and having my orders confirmed at the replacement center, I waited for the brigade to dispatch a jeep to pick me up. An hour later a red-haired private first class from the 199th Infantry Brigade walked into my tent and asked if I needed a ride to BMB. I had no idea what BMB stood for, so I asked him where we were going.

"Sir, we call our rear headquarters the Brigade Main Base, BMB. It's also called Camp Frenzell-Jones. Frenzell and Jones were the first two men from the 199th to be killed in action, and they named the camp after them."

"OK, let's get going," I replied.

As it turned out, the 199th main base was only a few miles north of the 90th Replacement Battalion. Ten minutes after departing the replacement battalion, the jeep turned right to enter the base camp of the 199th Light Infantry Brigade. A large sign near the main gate displayed the brigade patch and read "Camp Frenzell-Jones, 199th Light Infantry Brigade—Redcatchers." In smaller letters was the brigade's motto: Light, Swift, and Accurate.

The base camp sprawled over more than a thousand acres of rolling bare fields encircled by triple strands of barbed-wire fencing and thousands of rolls of concertina

11

wire. Sandbagged bunkers and observation towers dotted the landscape along the perimeter.

We drove slowly down the main dirt road past dozens of tents covered with a powdery orange dust stirred up by trucks, jeeps, and ACAVs (armored cavalry assault vehicles) moving along the camp's dirt roads. In one area, shirtless engineer troops constructed two-story, wood-frame barracks with corrugated tin roofs. The base camp was still a work in progress during the fall of 1967.

The driver stopped beside a makeshift wooden sidewalk that led to a group of large olive drab tents. I grabbed my duffel bag and followed the private up the sidewalk toward the brigade adjutant's tent. I took time to use a screen-covered barrel urinal outside the tent. Then I brushed the loose orange dust off my jungle fatigues and entered.

The adjutant sat in the rear of the tent behind a wooden field desk; he glanced up from a stack of paperwork as I entered. I presented a copy of my orders and my field personnel file to the sergeant at the front desk.

"Welcome to the 199th, Captain," he said. "You can go back and report to Major Kelley, the brigade adjutant."

Halting at the position of attention, three paces from the major's desk, I delivered the customary hand salute and formally reported: "Captain Tonsetic reporting for duty, Sir!"

The lanky crew-cut major squinted slightly as he gave me the once-over from behind his field desk.

"At ease, Captain. Welcome to the Redcatcher Brigade. We've been expecting you." The major stood to offer me a handshake and then gave me the standard five-minute briefing that he gave all incoming officers. He explained that the 199th was a separate light infantry brigade commanded by Brig. Gen. Robert Forbes. The brigade commander reported directly to the II Field Force commander. The brigade has a headquarters company, three infantry battalions, one artillery battalion, one combat support battalion, and an armored cavalry troop. He further explained that the brigade had been in-country for one year and was currently involved in Operation Fairfax, an operation to defend the Saigon-Bien Hoa-Long Binh areas against ground, mortar, and rocket attack.

Major Kelley then asked the personnel sergeant for my field 201 file. He closely examined the form that listed my previous assignments and school attendance.

"I see you're a Special Forces officer, Tonsetic; why do you suppose the Army didn't assign you to the 5th Special Forces Group?" He asked with a sardonic smile.

"Sir, I requested an infantry assignment. Infantry is my basic branch, and I want to command an infantry company." I sensed that this West Pointer wasn't too impressed with Green Beret officers.

"Well, we don't assign newly arrived captains as company commanders, especially Special Forces captains. You've been away from regular infantry troops for too long," Kelley continued.

"Sir, I served more than eighteen months as an infantry platoon leader before volunteering for Special Forces," I pointed out.

Smiling sternly the adjutant replied, "That was a while ago, Captain; I'm going to assign you to the brigade S-3 section. They might have something useful for you to do. You're going to have to prove yourself as a staff officer before you'll be considered for a command."

Sensing that the interview was about over, I saluted the major and replied, "Yes Sir, I understand!"

Major Kelley returned my salute and told me to go to the supply tent and draw an issue of jungle fatigues and field gear.

"One more thing, Captain. Cut that Special Forces patch off your uniform; you're a Redcatcher now," he grunted as he went back to his work.

After drawing my field gear and weapon, I made my way to the transient officers tent, where I joined about a dozen new officers, mostly lieutenants, who were packing their rucksacks in preparation to join their companies in the bush. Lieutenants and all enlisted soldiers had to complete a weeklong course at the Redcatcher academy before reporting to their units in the field. These lieutenants had just completed their training. I dumped my gear on an empty cot and set off to find the S-3 section.

The brigade tactical operations center (TOC), the main command-and-control element for the brigade, was located in a large, cavernous bunker near the center of the base camp. The brigade S-2 (intelligence) and S-3 (operations) staff shared the bunker. Artillery and Air Force liaison sections responsible for coordinating fire support for the brigade's deployed battalions also worked here. It was the nerve center for the brigade's operations, with a staff of nearly twenty personnel that included the staff officers, NCOs, and radio operators. The TOC maintained constant communications via FM radios and VHF communications. Large acetate-covered maps hung from the walls in the dimly lit bunker. Assorted military symbols indicating the locations of friendly positions and suspected enemy locations marked each map; red designated suspected enemy locations, and black represented friendly positions. Everybody was going about their work in a relaxed but businesslike manner, so I surmised that there wasn't much going on that afternoon.

I asked an operations sergeant where I could find the S-3, and he replied that Lieutenant Colonel Hall was at the brigade forward TOC at Cat Lai. He then directed me to a captain who was updating information on one of the situation maps.

"That's Captain Wilkinson over there, Sir; he's the assistant S-3 here at the brigade main TOC."

As I walked over and introduced myself to the captain, I noticed the armor branch insignia on his collar. Bob Wilkinson had been with the brigade for some time and knew the ins and outs of its operations. He spent about thirty minutes informally briefing me on the brigade's current operational status, pinpointing locations of the brigade's three infantry battalions. Each infantry battalion was deployed in what were considered to be enemy-threatened areas around the Capital Military District (CMD) of Saigon. The districts involved were Thu Duc, west of Saigon; Nha Be, southeast of Saigon along the Dong Nai River; and Binh Chanh, a few miles southwest of Saigon. All three battalions were working with the 5th Vietnamese Ranger Group, which was preparing to take over responsibility for the defense of the capital. After that was accomplished, Wilkinson said that the brigade would probably move north into War Zone D.

The captain finished his briefing and said that Lieutenant Colonel Hall wanted me to report to the forward deployed TOC at Cat Lai the following day.

"We fly a helicopter down there every morning with supplies. You can hitch a ride on it," Wilkinson suggested.

After a few questions, I thanked the amicable captain and headed back to the transient tent to pack my gear.

The next morning at 0700 I climbed aboard the UH-1 Huey supply bird for the flight to the brigade forward command post (CP) at Cat Lai, an old French seaplane base on the Saigon River east of the city. We flew south over flooded rice paddies that glistened in the morning sun. Muddy streams and canals flowed toward the larger watercourses. The end of the rainy season was near, and the water levels were down in the paddies and streams. Nipa palms and other thorny vegetation grew along the muddy banks of the undulating streams and rivers. As the UH-1 began its descent toward the small base at Cat Lai, I noticed two huge ocean-going freighters at anchor in the river near the shore.

"Those are ammunition ships," the pilot explained on the intercom. "I wouldn't want to be within ten miles of Cat Lai if the VC decide to blow up one of those ships."

The Huey descended over the orange tile roofs of the French colonial–period buildings and set down on the small helipad. I grabbed my rucksack and M16, jumped off the chopper, and made my way toward the largest building.

I found the S-3, Lt. Col. Ken Hall, in the operations section of the TOC. I liked this smiling, unpretentious officer immediately. He put me at ease, asked me where I was from back in the States, and explained that he was also new in-country. Just in from an assignment with the Infantry School at Fort Benning, he had arrived in Vietnam only a few days before me. Only a few lines around his eyes revealed the stress that he was now under. Brigade S-3 was the toughest job (other than battalion commander) that a lieutenant colonel could hold. As a very junior captain, I was still a bit on edge when conversing with officers a couple of grades above me, but I managed to ask a few questions about the brigade's current situation.

"We're going to send out a small group of officers to observe an ARVN [Army of the Republic of Vietnam] ranger operation in a couple of days," Hall said. "The general has to certify to the brass in Saigon that the rangers are ready to take over our mission around the capital before they'll release the brigade to go north," he explained.

"I'm sending out a major from the S-3 section on the ranger operation and I want you to go along, too. Good way for an infantry captain to get his feet wet. In more ways than one, that is," he added with a grin.

"Now go stow your gear in one of the tents out back, and I'll introduce you around when you get back. You'll get to meet the general tonight at our officers club," Hall said as he terminated the interview.

The club was in a high-ceilinged back room of the old

French villa that served as a makeshift headquarters. The room contained a few small tables and a larger round one, slow-moving ceiling fans, plenty of cigarette and cigar smoke, and a small bar in one corner. It was filled with officers coming off their twelve-hour day shifts in the TOC.

I ordered a beer at the bar and joined a table full of S-2 and S-3 officers, most of whom I'd met earlier in the day. About ten minutes later Lieutenant Colonel Hall arrived with a tall, broad-shouldered brigadier general in starched jungle fatigues with a single black star embroidered on each side of his collar.

The general was wearing spit-shined jungle boots that matched his shiny black leather general officer belt and holstered .32-caliber pistol. This was Brig. Gen. Robert Forbes, a distinguished-looking man in his early fifties with graying hair who looked every bit the general officer. He strode over to our table while Hall ordered two beers at the bar, and he seated himself before most of us could get to our feet.

"Sit down, sit down. Where's the dice cup? Anyone up for some Liars Dice?" Forbes asked.

The general produced a meerschaum pipe and tobacco pouch from his fatigue pockets, filled the bowl, lit the meerschaum, and glanced at the faces around the table, stopping at mine. "Captain, you must be new here. I don't recall your face."

Not used to conversing with general officers, I managed to stammer nervously, "Captain Tonsetic, General. I just reported in to the S-3 section."

"Welcome aboard, Captain. Good luck with that bunch of dog robbers in the S-3 section," he growled as he shook the dice cup.

Each time we rolled the dice, I had the impression that the general was sizing up each officer, trying to gauge our intellects and our tolerance for risk and audacity. The game continued longer than I anticipated. The general's enthusiasm for the game exceeded most of ours. After an hour and a half, and several beers, I excused myself to use the latrine and staggered back to my tent.

The next morning on my way back from the outdoor shower, I saw the general emerge from his air-conditioned trailer in a freshly pressed and starched set of fatigues. Trailed by his aide, he walked at a brisk pace toward his command-and-control (C&C) helicopter, a Huey that was settling toward the helipad. Forbes lived better than his staff officers, but as I was to learn over the next few months, he deeply cared for the soldiers in the brigade and placed their welfare above his own ambitions.

Brigadier General Robert C. Forbes had assumed command of the 199th Light Infantry Brigade two months earlier, when his predecessor, Brigadier General Freund, was seriously wounded during an airmobile operation. Forbes, a Pennsylvanian by birth, entered the Army in 1939 after graduating from the University of Pennsylvania. He served as an infantry officer in the European Theater during World War II, then had a succession of assignments that put him on the fast track to general officer rank. These included tours as secretary to the General Staff at the Pentagon, as an instructor at the Army's prestigious Command and General Staff College, and as an exchange officer at the British Staff College. Forbes was promoted to brigadier general in July 1966 and joined the 9th Infantry Division at Fort Riley, Kansas, as assistant division commander. He accompanied the division to Vietnam and later served as the chief of staff of II Field Force before assuming command of the Redcatcher Brigade in September 1967. He had all the right credentials to command a separate light infantry brigade.

chapter three
a long way from home

We are not about to send American boys nine or ten thousand miles away from home to do what Asian boys ought to be doing for themselves.

—LYNDON JOHNSON, 1964

A few days later, as brilliant sunlight began to burn off the morning mists, I stood on the muddy bank of the Saigon River with four other U.S. officers and a handful of radio operators waiting to board one of four large landing craft. More than three hundred Vietnamese army rangers, a full battalion, were gathered on the riverbank waiting to board the assault craft. Their officers and sergeants were shouting and pushing them onto the landing craft. The scene was one of absolute bedlam.

Most of the Vietnamese rangers were gangly boys in their late teens. They wore tight-fitting tiger-stripe fatigues and oversize U.S. steel helmets. They carried an assortment of vintage American World War II and Korean War weapons: M1 Garand rifles, Browning Automatic Rifles (BARs), and 57mm recoilless rifles, all too large and heavy for the average Vietnamese soldier.

Our small group of Americans made its way toward one of the rust-covered assault craft. The boat was about forty feet long by ten feet wide and was shaped like a topless shoe box with engines in the rear. We walked down the lowered ramp and into the troop well, where we sloshed through several inches of water that seeped through tiny crevices and cracks around the ramp. The troop well was packed with at least thirty rangers. Soldiers carrying their packs and rifles jostled each other to gain a few precious inches of space. I squeezed into a space near a bulkhead where I could brace my rucksack. The steady grind of the landing craft's motors muffled the high-pitched chattering of the Vietnamese. When the assault boat was filled to capacity, its motors grew louder and the pilot raised the ramp from the muddy river bank.

It was no more than half a mile across the river estuary. Perspiring, I stared at the boat's rusted brown steel hull and wondered what would happen when we landed on the far shoreline. Ten minutes later the sounds of the engines altered suddenly, and the landing craft shuddered to a stop. It took me a second to realize that we had landed.

After some delay, the ramp creaked and groaned downward onto the dark mud. An ugly slough of black mud about twenty yards wide to our front led into a dense tangle of nipa palms, roots, vines, and other foliage. Beyond the undergrowth was a vast expanse of flooded rice paddies.

The rangers in their oversize American helmets trudged down the ramp holding their ten-pound M1 rifles over their shoulders. They moved deftly across the mud slough, sinking in only up to their ankles, so I was surprised when I stepped off the ramp and immediately sank up to my knees in the stinking black muck. I was exhausted after moving about ten feet, straining to pull each foot out of the sucking, slimy mud. As I slowly cleared the mud slough, my thighs quivered with fatigue.

I glanced back over my shoulder and noticed that Maj. John Borgman, the brigade S-4 (logistics officer), was floundering waist deep in mud only a few yards from the shore. He was not moving forward at all, and the rangers moving around him were laughing as they passed. The assault craft was backing off the shoreline, so it was impossible for Borgman to go back.

I grabbed my radio operator's arm and told him that we had to help the major. We dropped our rucksacks and retraced our hard-earned steps. The major was carrying a bulging, overloaded rucksack and was obviously not prepared for this level of physical exertion. By the time we reached him, he was totally exhausted. He said that he had pulled a groin muscle and couldn't move. We pulled his overloaded rucksack off his back and tried to free him from the mud. It was a strenuous effort. The more he struggled, the deeper he sank. He was sweating profusely and his face had turned crimson. I recognized the symptoms of heat exhaustion, so I radioed for a helicopter evacuation.

It took about twenty minutes for the UH-1 to reach our location. With the aid of the crew chief, we managed to drag the major through the mud to the helicopter. By the time the Huey lifted off, the rear guard of the ranger battalion had moved almost five hundred meters ahead of us. My radio operator and I moved out to catch up.

It was an hour before we caught up with the rear of the ranger column. The battalion was halted along a long rice paddy dike. We were caked with black mud when we dropped to the ground, exhausted. I gulped several mouthfuls of water from my canteen as I scanned the panorama of paddies and dikes. I was angry at the Vietnamese and wondered what would happen if an American was wounded while accompanying a Vietnamese unit. Would they leave him behind to be captured or bleed to death alone in the paddies?

We continued our trek across the paddies, crossing numerous small canals and irrigation ditches. Farmers were noticeably absent in the rice fields that day. As noon approached, I could see several thatch roofs in a distant tree line.

We entered the village thirty minutes later; it was a small oasis in the rice paddies. A few old men in black pajamas squatted in front of their thatched huts while their sullen-looking women stood in the doorways, eyeing us apprehensively. Six or seven half-naked children scampered excitedly around the column as a dozen chickens and pigs fled in all directions. Several of the rangers broke ranks to chase after the villagers' scrawny chickens. Their noon meal would be chicken and rice.

Our group of six Americans halted outside the house in which the ranger commander had set up his command post. It was the largest and most prosperous-looking hooch in the small village. The Vietnamese commander's entourage of bat-boys, bodyguards, cooks, and staff officers had taken over the house and its dusty courtyard. Nylon hammocks appeared out of rucksacks and were strung in the shade for the officers while the cooks prepared a meal for the battalion commander and his staff.

As I updated the major from our brigade S-3 section about the helicopter evacuation of Major Borgman, I took note of the Ranger tab on his shoulder.

"I told him he was carrying too much shit," the major said. "He was just out here to justify applying for his Combat Infantry Badge."

The major then reminded us to keep notes on our impressions of the ARVN battalion. It was apparent he didn't think much of this unit.

"These guys are Saigon commandos. They're more interested in staging coups than killing VC. I was an advisor to a ranger outfit in II Corps and they'd run circles against this battalion."

The major looked in my direction. "Tonsetic, I want you to go check the security of the battalion perimeter."

I filled my canteen from a large earthenware jar beside the hooch and walked toward the edge of the village. Most of the troops built fires to boil their rice while their comrades sprawled in the shade. As I reached the perimeter, I noted that most of the rangers sat in small groups, smoking and chattering away with their buddies. It was more like a Sunday picnic in the park than a military operation.

"*Dai-uy, Dai-uy*, American cigarette?" the soldiers called as I walked by. "No VC, no VC!" they reassured me. Nobody seemed worried about anything.

It took about thirty minutes to walk the perimeter. The only security I noted was a few guards standing around listlessly as they stared outward into the rice paddies. When I returned to the ranger CP, I noticed that the ranger battalion commander was sprawled in a hammock taking a nap, as were all of his officers.

I reported my observations to the S-3 major, who shook his head disgustingly and said, "I thought as much. These Saigon commandos probably picked this area for their operation because they knew there weren't any VC within twenty miles."

I pulled a C ration can from my rucksack and joined the other U.S. officers. At about 1400, the ranger battalion commander rose from his nap and barked orders to his staff. Nervous radio operators relayed the orders to the company commanders. A few minutes later we resumed our march along the dikes. I never saw any of the Vietnamese soldiers give as much as a single piaster note to the villagers for the chickens and ducks they had eaten.

After three more hours of marching across seemingly endless rice paddies, we reached a much larger village with a small marketplace and several dozen houses, most with concrete floors and tile roofs. A Cao Dai temple dominated the other structures in the village.

The Vietnamese battalion commander selected a large house adjacent to the temple. It was a rectory of sorts where the holy men lived. The Cao Dai religious doctrine is rooted in both Buddhist and Christian theology, with strong overtones of Vietnamese folk religion. Among the "spiritual fathers" the Cao Dai pray to are Jesus, Buddha,

Confucius, and strangely enough, Sun Yat-sen and French writer-poet Victor Hugo. Like most faiths the Cao Dai have adopted a supreme symbol, the "Eye of God," a single staring eye that is painted on the walls of all their temples.

The Cao Dai disciples went about their business silently, completely ignoring our presence as we entered their house. We moved into a dining area with a twenty-foot-long mahogany table in the center. Benches that could be moved to the table lined the walls. I felt like an uninvited intruder but found a place on the floor where I laid my rucksack.

An hour later we were served a traditional Vietnamese dinner by a group of old Vietnamese women in black trousers and flowing white *ao dai*s. The first course was a clear soup with bean sprouts, celery, and other vegetables. Then the women brought a dish of meat and vegetables with hot green peppers, and a bowl of glutinous white rice. I dug a plastic C ration spoon from my pack after embarrassing myself with the chopsticks.

When the meal was over we spread our bedrolls on the concrete floor for the night. The place was eerie, but I drifted off to sleep exhausted from the day's march.

A few minutes before midnight I awoke to the sound of a loud gong. When I looked up, I saw a single file of white-robed old men with wispy beards moving past me in a ghostlike procession. They moved silently out the door and continued toward the adjacent temple. The sight thoroughly spooked me, and I rubbed my eyes to insure that I wasn't dreaming. I was unaware that the Cao Dai held four ceremonies daily, including one at midnight when God speaks to the believers through a medium. Suddenly, I felt very far from home in this strange land.

We departed the Cao Dai village at 0700. Around 1100, we were still slogging through the tepid water of the flooded paddies. The lead ranger company was about two hundred yards ahead of us, moving down a network of paddy dikes that led toward a tree line. I was carefully following a squad of rangers along a dike, trying to walk in their footsteps to avoid any mines or booby traps.

Suddenly, several sharp cracks sounded in the distance, followed by an equal number of *pop*s a foot or so above my head. These shots were immediately followed by a volley of rifle fire from the lead ranger company. I saw that the rangers had taken cover behind the paddy dikes and were firing into the tree line to their front. We were more than five hundred meters from the tree line, so I knew that we weren't within effective range for the snipers, but I still took cover behind the paddy dike.

Suddenly, about two dozen rangers in the lead company got to their feet and charged across the paddy toward the tree line. A VC machine gunner concealed in the trees fired a long burst at the assaulting troops. The rangers all dove into the mud, so I could not determine how many were hit.

The S-3 major, on the dike in front of me, radioed for gunship support. He was promised two of the new fully armed Cobra gunships in ten minutes. The attack helicopters were just completing a mission nearby.

The lead ranger company was pinned down by the machine-gun fire, unwilling to launch an assault on the clump of trees that concealed the enemy bunker. The ranger battalion commander was screaming orders into his radio handset, but none of his men were moving forward. The VC machine gunner continued to rake the ranger positions. Only sporadic rifle fire from the rangers answered the enemy machine gunner's bursts.

I glanced at the dike to my right and saw a couple of rangers trying to fire their .30-caliber light machine gun. The gun, a surplus U.S. weapon used in World War II and Korea, was jammed, and the rangers couldn't clear it.

The Cobra gunships finally arrived to break the stalemate.

After the major identified the enemy target and the position of the friendlies, the lead Cobra dove toward the bunker. Rounds from the gunship's roaring six-barrel, 7.62mm minigun slammed into the tree line at a rate of a hundred rounds per second.

As the lead Cobra came out of its run in a steep turn to the left, an intrepid Vietcong soldier popped out of a spider hole and cut loose on the gunship with a long burst from his AK-47. We saw the shark-nosed gunship shudder as it tried to gain altitude. Serious damage had been done to the Cobra. The pilot made a controlled emergency landing in the paddies on the other side of the tree line. His wingman dove on the tree line and punched off a salvo of rockets that silenced the machine gun. I later learned that we had witnessed the first shoot-down of an AH-1 Cobra gunship.

As soon as the machine gun was knocked out, the rangers were on their feet and assaulting the tree line. We followed them forward. The rangers pulled two dead VC from the bunker. Their limp forms were riddled with shrapnel wounds from the Cobra's 2.5-inch rockets.

We called a medevac for the ranger casualties and reminded the ranger battalion commander that he needed to send a unit to secure the downed gunship. Forty-five minutes later a CH-47 Chinook helicopter and a downed-aircraft recovery team arrived. Twenty minutes later, the damaged Cobra gunship was sling-lifted out of the muddy paddy beneath the Chinook.

It finally dawned on me after the skirmish that I'd actually seen action on the battlefield. Even though I had not fired a round, I had actually been under enemy fire for the first time.

Once the Cobra and its crew were safely evacuated, we moved out. Late in the afternoon we reached a paved road where a truck convoy waited to move the ranger battalion back to its base camp. The operation was over, and Major Jackson radioed for a helicopter to pick us up and fly us back to the brigade base at Cat Lai.

The following day the Americans who accompanied the battalion's operation drafted an evaluation report that was submitted to the S-3 and brigade commander. Our criticisms were a bit too blunt; the general said we had to tone down the report a bit before he could submit it to the Capital Military District (CMD) commander.

My opinion at that time was that if the rangers were some of the best troops that the South Vietnamese had to defend their own capital, they were in serious trouble. The rangers clearly needed additional training and modern weaponry before they would stand a fighting chance against main-force VC and NVA units.

Two weeks before Thanksgiving, Lieutenant Colonel Hall called me into his office to tell me that the brigade headquarters was leaving Cat Lai. The entire brigade was preparing to move north of Bien Hoa into War Zone D.

I assumed I'd stay with the brigade S-3 staff, but Hall told me that he needed a captain to run the Redcatcher Regional Force Training Center at Thu Duc. The brigade had established the training center to train Vietnamese Regional Force (RF) companies from Gia Dinh Province. The RFs were under the operational control of the Vietnamese district chiefs, and each company stayed in its own district to protect vital installations and conduct pacification operations. If the rangers were the elite troops, what would the RFs be like? The assignment didn't appeal to me, but I told Hall that I'd do the best job I could.

As it turned out, I enjoyed the training mission even though it was short lived. The training camp was only about seven miles from Camp Frenzell-Jones, and I had a small staff of one lieutenant and four sergeants. All had seen action in one of the brigade's infantry battalions; they were expert trainers. We had complete autonomy to develop the training program, and no one bothered us. Every two weeks an RF company would arrive at the camp to undergo the training.

Our training schedule included marksmanship, mines and demolitions, and small-unit tactics. The company undergoing training also secured our perimeter at night. The RF soldiers generally were enthusiastic and enjoyed the training cycle. At the end of each cycle, we held a graduation ceremony for the company, and Brigadier General Forbes always showed up to present training certificates to each RF soldier.

It was at one such ceremony, two days after Christmas 1967, that Forbes took me aside and asked me if I wanted to take command of an infantry company. I couldn't believe it. I had been in-country for only two months and had not yet served on an infantry battalion staff.

"Yes, Sir! That's what I wanted from the start."

"Good. Then I want you to fly up to Fire Support Base Nashua tomorrow and meet with Lt. Col. Bill Schroeder; he's commander of the 4th Battalion, 12th Infantry—the Warriors. We're going to have to shuffle the Warrior officers around a bit."

As Forbes's C&C helicopter lifted off our helipad, I stood there feeling dazed. I was happy and apprehensive at the same time. Suddenly, I felt a lack of confidence. Was I really ready to lead men in combat? Well, there was no turning back now, I concluded. My training team threw me a small party that night. Over some cold beers, I asked my lieutenant and sergeants hundreds of questions about what to expect when I went to the bush. I regretted having to leave them. They were great soldiers.

chapter four

meet the warriors

He saith among the trumpets, Ha, ha; and he smelleth the battle far off, the thunder of the captains, and the shouting.

—Job 39:24

January 1968

I stared out the Huey's door at the tangled mantle of patchy green and black jungle vegetation below as the helicopter descended toward the fire support base (FSB). Less than five miles south of the Song Be River, in the southern portion of War Zone D, FSB Nashua occupied the site of an old French military camp at the intersection of a network of narrow red-clay roads and logging trails. Fortified enemy base camps, supply depots, and way stations lay hidden in the surrounding jungle, protected by battle-hardened veterans of the VC Dong Nai Regiment. War Zone D was a major staging area for Communist assault units on their way to Bien Hoa and Long Binh, and FSB Nashua was the forward 199th Brigade base for intercepting these VC and NVA units.

Nashua was larger than I expected; it sprawled over more than sixty acres of flat terrain. The jungle around the fire base perimeter had been pushed back by bulldozers and sprayed with defoliants. Each of the Warrior battalion's four rifle companies defended a portion of the Nashua perimeter. Coils of concertina wire were strung in front of heavily sandbagged bunkers spaced thirty to fifty yards apart on each

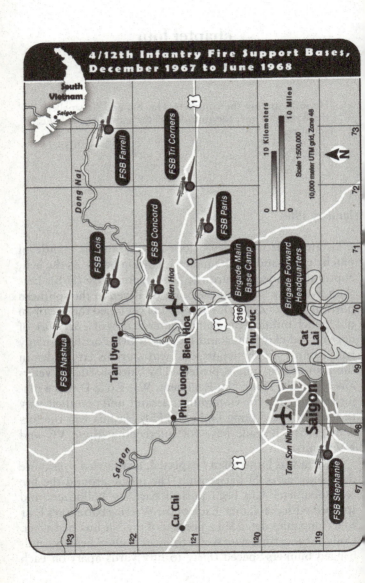

4/12th Infantry Fire Support Bases, December 1967 to June 1968

South Vietnam
Saigon

FSB Farrell
FSB Tri Corners
FSB Paris
FSB Concord
FSB Lois
FSB Nashua
FSB Stephanie

Dong Nai
Bien Hoa

Brigade Main Base Camp
Brigade Forward Headquarters

Tan Uyen
Phu Cuong
Bien Hoa
Thu Duc
Cat Lai
Cu Chi
Saigon
Tan Son Nhut

10 Kilometers   10 Miles
0   0
Scale 1:500,000
10,000 meter UTM grid, Zone 48

N

side of the perimeter. A troop of ACAVs reinforced the perimeter with the firepower of their .50-caliber and 7.62mm machine guns. Beyond the perimeter lay a cleared no-man's-land, and beyond that was thick secondary jungle growth. Within the perimeter sat a battery of 105mm howitzers, a large sandbagged bunker housing the battalion TOC, an aid station, and an assortment of other support units.

I arrived at FSB Nashua on 1 January 1968, to assume command of Charlie Company, 4th Battalion, 12th Infantry. December 1967 had been a bloody month for the Warrior battalion.

The battalion had moved north from Thu Duc to Nashua on 4 December and fought a costly battle two days later. Two platoons from Alpha Company were ordered to find and destroy the enemy mortar sites that had been firing on Nashua. The Warrior platoons, unaccustomed to maneuvering in dense jungle, stumbled into an enemy base camp, which triggered a bloody daylong battle. Casualties were heavy: twenty-one KIA and seventy-four WIA, the heaviest since the unit's arrival in Vietnam in December 1966.

Reinforced by a company of the 3d Battalion, 7th Infantry, and a platoon from Delta Troop, 17th Cavalry, the Warrior battalion finally turned the tide and overran the enemy base camp on the morning of 7 December. Troops entering the enemy camp reported finding 67 enemy dead strewn among the 125 heavily fortified bunkers. They also found several friendly KIAs in the enemy trenches. These men had been shot, execution-style, in the back of the head. The Warriors were even more outraged when they found the mutilated corpse of one of their lieutenants hanging by a rope from a tree. He had been wounded and captured early in the fight and then apparently tortured to death. His body was then hung in the tree to taunt the U.S. soldiers—a despicable and cowardly atrocity.

It was during this battle that Catholic Chaplain Angelo

Liteky earned the Medal of Honor. Liteky was credited with carrying more than twenty men to an LZ for evacuation during the savage fighting. More bloody fights occurred on 12 and 26 December. The 26 December fight brought about my command of Charlie Company.

Charlie Company left Nashua on a reconnaissance-in-force operation on the morning of 26 December and stumbled into an enemy ambush. The point platoon leader, his radio operator, and another soldier were killed. Ten others were wounded as the company struggled to fight its way out of the kill zone.

The company commander was badly shaken and unable to control the unit, so the company first sergeant had to take temporary control of the fight. After several minutes of confused and bitter fighting, the battalion commander, circling overhead in his C&C ship, ordered the 3d Platoon leader, Lt. Paul Viola, to take command of the company. The battle raged on until Delta Company arrived on the scene to reinforce Charlie Company. The outnumbered VC force withdrew into the jungle.

After the 26 December battle, the Warrior commander, Lt. Col. Bill Schroeder, decided to replace the Charlie Company commander. He consulted with Brigadier General Forbes, who recommended me for the job; this bypassed another eligible captain on Schroeder's staff.

I reported to the battalion commander and received an update on the unit's situation. It wasn't good. Replacements for the men lost in the December battles were slow in coming, and a siege mentality had overtaken the troops at Nashua. A certain shock trauma spread through the ranks, and the men dreaded leaving the fire base. They had not yet adjusted to the changes of terrain in the new area of operations (AO), nor to the tactics employed by the main-force VC units. For a year they had plodded through open rice paddies and were opposed mainly by small local VC units. Now they were in the jungle facing highly trained and disciplined main-force enemy battalions that knew how to use the ground to their advantage.

Schroeder was a tough and focused commander, and he was clearly frustrated that his battalion had been so badly bloodied in the December fights. He was nearing the end of his six-month command tour and wanted the battalion to regain the initiative. After the briefing, Schroeder escorted me to the Charlie Company CP bunker on the western side of the perimeter. The change of command was an unceremonious affair. Schroeder introduced me to the outgoing commander, we shook hands, and the captain picked up his rucksack and strode off with the battalion commander. A handful of troops sitting atop a nearby bunker looked on impassively.

The imposing six-foot-three Charlie Company first sergeant walked over and introduced himself.

"I'm the company first sergeant, George Holmes, Sir," he said as he gazed at the two departing officers.

"Good to meet you, Top," I responded while noting the star on his Combat Infantry Badge. Holmes had seen combat in Korea, too. "What's going on with Charlie Company today?"

"Not a goddamn thing, Captain, but we need to talk before I take you around to meet the platoon leaders and platoon sergeants."

Over a canteen cup of C ration coffee, the first sergeant filled me in on Charlie Company, emphasizing how my predecessor had lost control of himself in the firefight five days earlier.

"I told the battalion commander that he had to go; he should have taken him out that same day," Holmes explained as he filled me in on the details of the action.

"The men lost all confidence in him; I told the battalion

sergeant major and the colonel that he had to go. Don't know why in the hell they waited a week."

"How's the morale of the troops?" I asked.

"Piss poor, Captain! We got our asses kicked good last week. These guys are really spooked. Every time we go outside the wire, we end up getting the worst of it."

"Well, what do we need to do to bring them out of it, Top?"

"For starters they need a swift kick in the ass. Then they need to see some dead VC. In most of these fights, the VC didn't leave many dead behind. The body counts battalion reported were pure bullshit. I know we got some, but these Commie bastards are disciplined troops, and they don't leave their dead and wounded behind."

Holmes was right; the platoon leaders and senior NCOs confirmed it. More than anything else, the men wanted a chance to even the score, but at that point they had lost all confidence in themselves and their leaders. I hoped that I could change that.

Charlie Company was a light infantry rifle company that was organized into three rifle platoons and a mortar platoon with three 81mm mortars. Each rifle platoon was led by a lieutenant platoon leader assisted by an E-7 or E-6 platoon sergeant. The platoon was further organized into three rifle squads and an M60 machine-gun squad, each led by an E-5 buck sergeant. Most of these squad leaders were draftees who had earned their rank in Vietnam. On paper, the company was supposed to have around 160 men, but our field strength rarely reached 120 men. Casualties, R&R leaves, and a less-than-adequate replacement stream always kept the rifle companies below their authorized strength. The average Charlie Company soldier was an unmarried twenty-year-old draftee with a high-school education, although some had college experience.

A small command group consisting of me, the first sergeant, two radio-telephone operators (RTOs), a field supply sergeant, a medic, and an attached artillery forward observer (FO) with his recon sergeant provided for the command-and-control and logistic support to the rifle and mortar platoons. We also kept a small detachment at the main base camp led by the company executive officer (XO), a senior lieutenant. The XO supervised a rear detachment sergeant, senior supply sergeant, a company clerk, a jeep driver, and others. This group kept the supplies and mail going forward, prepared the morning reports and casualty reports, wrote award recommendations, and supervised soldiers joining the company, leaving for R&R, and out-processing to go home.

Our weaponry included the M16 rifle, the M79 grenade launcher, the M60 machine gun, and the mortar platoon's three 81mm mortars. The company also had 90mm recoilless rifles, but these antitank weapons were usually left in the rear due to their weight. We had one jeep assigned to the company. The jeep always stayed in the rear and was used for supply and administrative purposes.

I knew from the start that I would have to rely heavily on my first sergeant. With seventeen years of infantry experience behind him, including combat experience in Korea, Holmes was the most respected soldier in the company. He looked the part. At thirty-three years, he was a muscular six-foot-three man with a deeply tanned face and tattooed forearms. With his imposing stature and deep, resonant voice, this son of a career marine had no difficulty getting the troops' attention. As a younger NCO, Holmes had served a tour in the 3d Infantry, Old Guard, at Fort Meyer, guarding the Tomb of the Unknown Soldier. Before that he had cut his teeth with the 25th Infantry Division in Hawaii in 1951. Later that year he deployed to Korea, where he joined the 45th Infantry Division. Holmes spent his first night in combat on Old Baldy where, though wounded, he was among a handful of survivors of a massive Chinese artillery bombardment and human-wave attack. A little over a decade later he volunteered for his first tour in Vietnam and served as a CH-21 helicopter door gunner, there being no U.S. ground troops in-country at that time. Holmes believed that a first sergeant belonged in the field with the troops, and even though he had been with the company for only a month, he knew all its strengths and weaknesses.

For the next three days, Charlie Company stayed in a defensive posture at FSB Nashua. Rumors spread that the battalion was scheduled to move south toward Bien Hoa. I used the time to speak with each of my lieutenants and platoon sergeants about the company. Lieutenant Paul Viola, the 3d Platoon leader, recorded in his pocket notebook the following issues, which I discussed with him: cleaning and test firing of weapons on a daily basis, fire plans for his platoon's sector, communications discipline, personal hygiene including shaving in the field, getting rid of complacency, and ambush tactics.

Each platoon leader also walked me around his area and introduced me to some of the men. A few stand out in my memory: Doc Poole, a combat medic from Hope, Arkansas; Vito Graziano, a tough youth from the streets of New York City; Mike Tuszl, a tall, blond Californian; and Allen Pollastrini from the coal-mining town of Fairfield, West Virginia. The Warriors of Charlie Company were a cross section of the best America had to offer.

On 5 January the battalion moved to an area south of the Dong Nai River to the east of Bien Hoa. This was part of a larger plan by the II Field Force commander, Gen. Frederick Weyand, to move a number of U.S. battalions out of the remote jungle and border areas and back toward populated areas. Weyand believed that an enemy offensive directed against South Vietnam's population centers was coming.

Charlie Company was ordered to board helicopters to fly south to FSB Concord, northeast of Bien Hoa. Our new mission was to provide security for the battalion headquarters and its direct-support artillery battery at Concord, and to serve as the brigade ready-reaction force. This latter mission meant that we had to be ready to move two platoons on fifteen minutes' notice, day or night, to any hotspot in the brigade AO. The company would be allocated ten UH-1 sorties if the reaction was to be by air.

I was surprised that the battalion commander assigned this mission to Charlie Company, because I was his least-experienced company commander. His decision strengthened my determination to uphold the trust he had placed in me.

Concord sat atop a ridgeline overlooking the Dong Nai River. Clearly visible across the river was the southernmost portion of War Zone D, an area known as the "rocket belt." It was from this area that the enemy bombarded the U.S. bases at Bien Hoa and Long Binh with their deadly accurate 122mm rockets. The artillery at FSB Concord was on call to fire counter-battery missions against the 122mm rocket-firing sites.

Rocket attacks were not the only threat to the Bien Hoa and Long Binh bases, however. As we soon found out, enemy ground troops used the jungle and rubber plantations surrounding the fire base to infiltrate and stage for ground attacks on the nearby U.S. air and logistic bases.

Two days after moving to Concord, the Warrior battalion welcomed a new commander. Lieutenant Colonel Bill Mastoris replaced Schroeder, who had completed his six-month command tour. Mastoris was a quiet, even-tempered, scholarly looking West Pointer. He made no immediate changes in the battalion. Instead he relied heavily on his S-3, Maj. Ed King, to run the battalion's day-to-day operations. We all hoped our new commander's learning curve wouldn't be too steep in the days ahead.

After Charlie Company arrived at Concord, I began to think about our brigade ready-reaction mission. As yet, I had never had a chance to maneuver the company on a field operation. I also had a new platoon leader in 1st Platoon, Howard Tuber, age twenty-two, and fresh out of Fort Benning Officer Candidate School. We both needed some experience with the company in the bush before deploying on any ready-reaction missions, which always held a high probability of enemy contact. I went to Mastoris and asked if Charlie Company could be assigned some short-duration operations near Concord. He agreed, and over the next couple of weeks I had the opportunity to deploy two platoons at a time on several overnight operations into the rocket belt.

Deploying by helicopter, we would land north of the Dong Nai River and conduct daylight sweeps before setting up a night defensive position (NDP) in the jungle. We made no contact with the enemy, but found plenty of abandoned bunkers and rice caches.

In mid-January our battalion began to receive intelligence reports indicating that the enemy was up to something big. The S-2 briefed us that VC main force units were moving west to east in the area north of the Dong Nai River, and then continuing south to cross the river and infiltrate the Bien Hoa area. The credibility of these reports received a boost when a ground-surveillance radar section on the Concord perimeter reported movement through an adjacent valley during darkness. When the radar detected movement, we fired our mortars at the designated coordinates. We also sent night ambush patrols into the valley, but the enemy managed to elude the patrols.

When not on operation, the troops lived well on the fire base. They had hot mess-hall chow, cold beer and soda, and showers. First Sergeant Holmes suggested that we send a half-platoon at a time into the city of Bien Hoa for a half-day of R&R. Half the platoon would go in the morning, the other half in the afternoon. Holmes referred to the excursions as "pussy runs."

"Okay, Top," I replied. "But tell the sergeants that if anyone is late in returning, I'll cancel the runs. Also, the guilty party gets an Article 15."

"No sweat, Captain. If anyone misses his ride, the guys in his own platoon will kick his ass for screwing up the program."

We had our first real opportunity to deploy on a brigade ready-reaction mission on 27 January. Shortly after midnight, Major King alerted me that a brigade long range reconnaissance patrol (LRRP) was in contact with a small VC force just north of the village of Ho Nai, which was just north of the BMB camp at Long Binh.

We left Concord fifteen minutes later mounted on five ACAVs from Delta Troop, 17th Armored Cavalry. By the time we linked up with the LRRPs in a small cemetery just north of the village, the skirmish was over. The LRRPs had ambushed what was apparently a small VC reconnaissance patrol. We dismounted the ACAVs and swept through the cemetery under artillery illumination flares. We found one body. The dead VC was clad in black pajamas and carried an American .45-caliber pistol, binoculars, and lensatic compass. He was probably an officer or a scout. After a thorough search of the area, we mounted up and returned to Concord blithely unaware of the significance of this mission.

chapter five
the tet offensive

O God of battles! Steel my soldiers' hearts;
Possess them not with fear; take from them now
The sense of reckoning, if the opposed numbers
Pluck their hearts from them.
                                                        —WILLIAM SHAKESPEARE,
                                                        Henry V

The Tet Offensive

The weeklong Vietnamese holiday of Tet, a celebration of the lunar new year, began on 31 January. In Vietnam, Tet is the major religious, patriotic, and family holiday period of the year. Although a cease-fire had been agreed upon by the North and South Vietnamese, it was canceled prior to the holiday. We were informed of these developments at a midmorning briefing on 30 January. Our brigade, along with other U.S. forces, were promptly ordered to maximum alert. Unfortunately, the bulk of the Vietnamese military personnel had already returned to their homes for family reunions and celebrations and could not be immediately recalled. Celebration plans for the holiday continued among the South Vietnamese.

The holiday had a direct impact on Charlie Company, one that I didn't like. Because most of the Vietnamese military was on leave, Charlie Company picked up some additional security missions. I was ordered to provide one platoon during the hours of darkness for the defense of a POW camp located between Bien Hoa and Long Binh. I assigned this mission to 1st Platoon under Lt. Howard Tuber. I was also ordered to dispatch a squad to defend a dredge site on the

Dong Nai River south of Bien Hoa. This left the company seriously undermanned. The battalion commander also ordered Charlie Company to deploy 2d Platoon, less the squad on the dredge site, to an ambush site in the valley east of the fire base each night. Consequently, on the night of 31 January, I had only 3d Platoon and Mortar Platoon to defend FSB Concord. I was very concerned that Charlie Company was overextended with these various missions.

My concerns fell on deaf ears at Battalion. The battalion S-3 said that the rear-echelon troops at Concord would just have to move to the bunker line and defend the base if Charlie Company received a ready-reaction deployment order from Brigade. All of us thought that this wouldn't happen. We couldn't have been more wrong.

Ho Nai, 30–31 January

The evening of 30 January was deceptively quiet around FSB Concord. I watched as Lt. Al Lenhardt's 2d Platoon slipped through the wire in the evening twilight and headed for their night ambush location. The men had blackened their faces and were traveling without rucksacks; they carried only weapons and ammo. Steel helmets were replaced with soft jungle hats. The 1st Platoon had departed some hours earlier for their night mission at the POW compound. Walking over to Mortar Platoon's location, I checked to ensure that they'd plotted defensive concentrations (DEFCONs) in support of the 2d Platoon ambush. These fires would be on call if the patrol requested them. Lieutenant Paul Viola, newly designated platoon leader for the mortars, and PSgt. Cliff Jaynes sat in the platoon's fire direction center bunker.

"Did you get Lenhardt squared away on his defensive fires?" I asked.

"Yes, Sir. He's in good shape. All he has to do is call, and the rounds will be on the way in seconds," Viola responded.

"We still have our other mission, the ready-reaction force. I'm going to have to deploy most of your platoon if we get the order to move. You'll deploy as a rifle platoon if we get called out. I want you to keep one gunner here on each mortar tube, three men in all, and a couple of guys in the fire direction center."

Platoon Sergeant Jaynes remained silent during my conversation with Viola. Jaynes, a twelve-year veteran of the regular Army, was reputed to be the best mortar platoon sergeant in the brigade. I had served as a mortar platoon leader as a lieutenant; it was obvious to me that Jaynes knew what he was doing.

"We can handle it, Sir," Jaynes finally said, ending his silence.

I left the bunker and returned to my CP, where I tried to calculate my rifle strength if we did get called out. Somewhere around forty, I figured.

Lying on my cot at the CP, I tried to read a *Stars and Stripes*. Holmes was also stretched out snoring. I soon dozed off. Only my two radio telephone operators (RTOs), SP/4 Cliff Kaylor, a blond-haired Ohioan with a sunburned face and a rolling Midwest accent, and SP/4 Bob Archibald, an easygoing twenty-one-year-old Californian, remained dutifully awake and made periodic commo (communication) checks with 1st Platoon at the POW compound and Lenhardt's ambush patrol.

A few minutes before midnight, a runner from the battalion TOC woke me. He relayed a message that a LRRP had radioed in a sighting of eighty VC near the cemetery where we had deployed three nights earlier. Colonel Fred Davison, commanding the 199th while Brigadier General Forbes was on leave, wanted us to check it out. Here we go again, I thought, suspicious of the numbers of enemy that the LRRPs reported. As it turned out, I was dead wrong.

Three miles to the east of FSB Concord, Specialist 5th Class Vincent's six-man LRRP team lay hidden in the brush, trying to count heads in a long VC column passing by their position. The enemy troops moved quickly down a dirt road leading south from the Dong Nai River toward the village of Ho Nai. The team had stopped counting at eighty and radioed in their report. More VC were coming, and they were heavily armed with assault rifles, heavy and light machine guns, shoulder-fired rocket launchers, and mortars.

Meanwhile, FSB Concord had become a beehive of activity. Battalion headquarters troops, roused from their bunkers inside the perimeter, rushed to the defensive bunkers along the perimeter while Charlie Company soldiers assembled near the ACAVs, which were lining up in column formation. The infantrymen and cavalrymen were none too happy about going out on another mission. Unbeknownst to me, some partying had been going on at the fire base earlier that evening.

Holmes took a quick headcount. "Captain, we've got thirty-eight men total for the mission, not counting the cav guys."

"Well, let's mount 'em up, Top."

As I climbed aboard the lead track, I noticed Lieutenant Viola standing beside me. I made a hasty decision.

"Lieutenant, you've got to stay here," I shouted over the tracks' idling engines. "I want you to stay with your mortars and take charge of the troops on the perimeter. I've got to leave an officer in charge here."

The disappointed lieutenant headed back to the bunker line. Leaving Viola behind meant that I'd have no platoon leaders on the mission. First Sergeant Holmes would be second in command. The 3d Platoon was led by PSG Orville Wyers. Lieutenant Bob Stanley, the regular platoon leader, was on R&R. Wyers, thirty-four, joined the Army at seventeen and made NCO rank before Vietnam. The Wisconsin native was a newcomer to Charlie Company. PSG Jaynes was leading the Mortar Platoon grunts, who were deploying as a rifle platoon.

We clambered aboard the tracks and tried to find a few inches of cramped space on the decks. No one rode in the troop compartments, which were filled with ammo boxes. If the track ran over a mine or took an RPG (rocket-propelled grenade) hit, troops were better off dismounting from the deck or even being blown off. Even with seven ACAVs, the infantrymen had to squeeze into every square inch on top of the tracks. Looking back at the other ACAVs, I saw that one had a 106mm recoilless rifle mounted on the deck. That recoilless rifle, along with the ACAVs' .50-caliber machine guns, could prove decisive in a firefight, I thought. On the other hand, ACAVs were big, noisy targets for the enemy. We weren't going to surprise the enemy; they'd hear us coming a mile off.

When I saw that Charlie Company was mounted, I signaled my track commander to move out. The seven ACAVs lurched forward, leaving a trail of dust behind. It was a clear night and relatively cool.

The first checkpoint on our route was a junction where the road from Concord intersected with Highway 1 in a stand of rubber trees five kilometers south of the fire base. I radioed our location to the TOC as the column neared the road junction. Mastoris ordered me to halt the column at the intersection and stand by for further orders.

I signaled the track commander, and the ACAVs rolled to a stop. Then I ordered my platoons to dismount and form a 360-degree perimeter around the tracks.

The rubber plantation was pitch-black and eerily silent, except for the idling engines of the tracks. Minutes later the thundering roar of a 122 mm rocket salvo streaking across

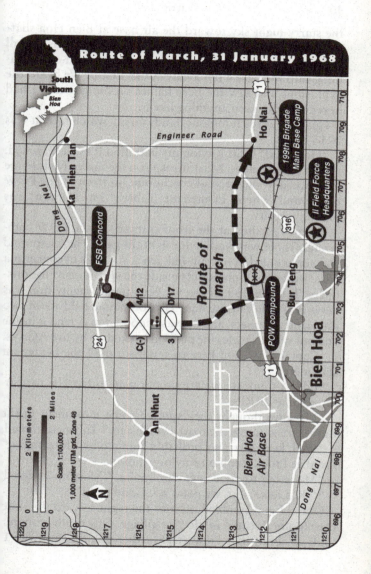

Route of March, 31 January 1968

the starry night sky toward the air base at Bien Hoa shattered the silence. They sounded like freight trains at full throttle. The first rockets hit their targets dead-on, slamming into the base's JP4 aviation fuel dump. We heard the explosions and saw the fiery flames on the horizon. I had never heard or seen anything like it.

I glanced at the luminous hands on my watch face. It was 0215 hours.

"Holy shit!" Cliff Kaylor, my battalion RTO, exclaimed.

Shortly thereafter, Mastoris was on the radio. He told me to proceed to our second checkpoint, in front of the POW compound where Lieutenant Tuber's 1st Platoon was pulling security.

When we halted at the front entrance to the POW compound, Tuber was waiting for us at the gate. The compound was surrounded by a chain-link fence and rolls of concertina wire. Rows of Quonset huts inside the wire housed the prisoners. Tuber, who had not yet been under enemy fire, was nervous. I didn't blame him. The compound held about two thousand prisoners, and he was supposed to defend it inside and out with a single rifle platoon backed up by five ACAVs.

"Captain, are you here to reinforce us?" the lieutenant stammered.

"I don't think so; we are on our way to Ho Nai to reinforce some LRRPs."

"My guys thought they spotted some movement in the rubber trees across the road a while ago," Tuber continued.

"Well, keep alert; it's probably going to be a long night," I said as I took a call on Kaylor's radio.

"Move out to your next checkpoint," Mastoris ordered.

"OK, Lieutenant, we gotta go. Good luck!"

Our column rumbled off into the night toward the third checkpoint, located in Ho Nai village. Our route of march took us about four kilometers farther east on Highway 1 past the turnoff to Highway 316, which led south toward Saigon. Houses and small shops lined the highway east of the rubber plantation. Because it was well past curfew, we stopped to pick up a suspicious-looking Viet who was walking along the highway. The man had no ID card, so we took him with us. As we continued, I thought I heard the sound of firecrackers going off among the houses to the sides of the road. Tet celebrants, I reassured myself.

We passed a Vietnamese hospital and Catholic church and rolled into the center of Ho Nai village toward our next checkpoint. I knew the location from three nights before; it was the intersection where the dirt road turned north off Highway 1 toward the Dong Nai River. When we reached the checkpoint, I ordered the tracks to halt so the Charlie Company troops could dismount.

I noticed that Bob Archibald, one of my RTOs, was limping badly after we dismounted.

"Archibald, what's wrong with your leg?" I asked.

"I think I twisted my ankle jumping off the track."

"Well, grab someone else to carry that radio then. I need someone who can keep up. You stay with Top."

Next I called First Sergeant Holmes, my two platoon sergeants (Jaynes and Wyers), and the armored cavalry platoon leader for some quick instructions.

"We're going to take it slow from here," I said. "We're going to move up the dirt road toward the cemetery with Wyers's 3d Platoon to the left of the road and Jaynes's 4th Platoon on the right. Keep off the road itself. Try to stay low in those ditches on each side of the road.

"Lieutenant," I said, addressing the cavalry officer, "I want your tracks to move up the road about fifty meters behind my platoons.

"Top, I'll follow 3d Platoon on the left with my RTOs. You move near the rear with the rest of the CP group.

"Anybody have any questions?" I asked. No one spoke up.

"Okay then. We move out in five," I said as I stared down the road.

I tried to raise the LRRPs on their radio frequency, but there was no answer. All was quiet to our front.

We started moving north on both sides of the road. Specialist Nick Schneider, a seasoned veteran from the Bronx, led the point squad from 3d Platoon on the left, following the knee-deep drainage ditch. The ground sloped gently downward for about four hundred meters toward a small stream on the low ground. A culvert ran under the road at that point. Beyond the streambed and culvert, the ground rose sharply over the steep banks of the watercourse and then sloped gently upward. The small cemetery where the LRRPs had killed the VC three nights before was on the east side of the road about fifty meters beyond the streambed.

About forty meters ahead of Schneider's point man, two figures darted across the darkened road and disappeared into the brush. We all saw them at the same time. I thought they might be men from the LRRP patrol or the village's Popular Forces (PF) platoon. Suddenly, someone—possibly one of the cavalry troopers—popped a hand flare, which lit up the night sky.

Schneider later reported that "When the flare went off, we saw several figures run across the road to our front, but we weren't close enough to tell who they were." Moving forward, he suddenly saw a tripod-mounted machine gun sitting on the side of the road in front of the culvert. Still believing it might belong to the PF troops, he moved closer until he recognized that the gun was a Chinese 12.75mm machine gun. No enemy manned the gun at that moment. Schneider shouted for his point man to take cover.

Specialist Ken Barber, an alert nineteen-year-old Virginian, reacted instinctively when he spotted three VC crawling out of the roadside ditch to put the gun into action. Blasting away with his pump-action shot gun, Barber killed all three before they could load the heavy machine gun. The remainder of the squad began firing into the darkness to their front. Dozens of muzzle flashes answered their fire.

Wyers's 3d Platoon pressed the attack on the left of the road while Jaynes's men inched up the drainage ditch to close with the action across the road. All hell was breaking loose. The ACAVs rumbled forward to join the fray.

Schneider's men advanced until they spotted a group of thirty to forty VC scrambling across the stream and rushing toward our left flank. Realizing that the VC were trying to flank his platoon, Schneider quickly opened fire with his M16. He blazed away on full automatic and quickly expended two magazines. Then he heaved three grenades toward the enemy and ran back to the lead track to retrieve his rucksack in which he carried more ammo and grenades.

The assaulting VC reeled under the fire from Schneider's squad and moved farther from the road to outflank us. They ran into an unexpected obstacle.

A few months earlier, Army engineers had dug sand and dirt from an area about twenty meters from the road, creating a steep embankment. The VC ran straight into it. A few managed to scramble up the bank, but most of them didn't make it. The lead ACAV, now on line with 3d Platoon, opened up on the trapped VC with its .50-caliber and 7.62mm machine guns, cutting them to ribbons. This group of VC was trapped in a slaughter pen with no way out.

Observing the plight of their comrades, an enemy RPG team hidden in a hooch off the right side of the road took aim at the lead ACAV. Schneider had just retrieved his rucksack from the vehicle and was hustling back to his squad when the RPG round struck the right side of the track,

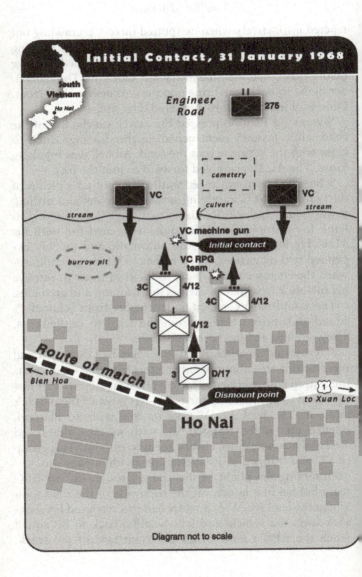

Initial Contact, 31 January 1968

starting a fire in the fuel compartment. The four crewmen jumped off the burning vehicle. Three sustained shrapnel wounds from the RPG.

The crewmen joined Jaynes's troops, who were hunkered down in the drainage ditch along the right side of the road. Jaynes had spotted the RPG team firing from the house and ordered his men to take the hooch under fire. Tracer and M79 rounds set the thatched roof on fire, but not before the VC got off another rocket. This round slammed into the next vehicle in the column, inflicting serious damage. The remaining five tracks tried to withdraw. They were sitting ducks on the narrow road and could move safely only in reverse. The road was too narrow for turning around.

When we started taking fire, I was walking by a house to the left of the road, about forty yards behind Schneider's lead squad. I dove for cover beside a dilapidated old truck parked nearby and looked around for the RTO who had replaced Archibald.

The RTO had crawled under the truck and was paralyzed with fear. I couldn't get the radio handset from him. Kaylor was on the battalion radio next to me, calling for fire support.

Suddenly, I realized how exposed we were. I spotted three or four dark silhouettes as they darted between the deserted hooches to my left. This small group of VC had managed to climb the steep embankment and escape the slaughter pen.

Shit, they're flanking us, I thought as I squeezed off a couple of shots at them from my CAR15. I was still screaming at my RTO under the truck as Kaylor and I fired off another couple bursts at the AK-47 muzzle flashes in the darkness.

My weapon jammed, and I couldn't clear it. I pulled a grenade off my harness and hurled it over the roof of the house and into the garden in the rear, and I followed it up with a second grenade. I grabbed my company RTO by the harness and dragged him out from under the truck while Kaylor made contact with the artillery. I had no idea what happened to my FO and his recon sergeant at this point. They were nowhere near me.

"Sir, the arty won't fire within a hundred meters of the village and they'll only give us one tube. They've prioritized on the rocket sites across the Dong Nai," Kaylor shouted.

"Damn it. Then call in a fire mission on the high ground on the other side of the culvert."

Schneider made it back to his squad before he took some shrapnel from another RPG. Third Platoon's sergeant Orville Wyers and Sgt. Ronny Simons were also hit, but they were still in the fight. I could tell from the cries for medics that we had other men hit as well, but I had no idea how many.

While the house across the road was aflame, I remained concerned that the RPG team was still in action. The ACAV with the 106mm recoilless rifle was backing up the road a few meters from me. I yelled at the track commander to fire on the house, but I couldn't get his attention. Seconds later, the thatch roof of the house was fully ablaze and caved into the house. When the flames engulfed the VC stash of ammunition inside the house, the whole structure exploded outward. I felt a blast of hot air and my ears rang from the explosion.

Wyers's men from 3d Platoon pulled back with their wounded. Specialists Alonzo Shelton, Ken Barber, and Pfc. Dale Reidenga laid down a base of fire to cover the platoon's withdrawal. The less-seriously wounded were assisting those with more-serious wounds. Specialists Lester Brown, James Hayward, Terrance Miller, and Jerold Partch, along with Privates First Class Bille and Matlaw—six of the most experienced grunts in 3rd Platoon—were among the wounded.

I couldn't see any of Jaynes's 4th Platoon troops in the darkness on the other side of the road. They crouched in the drainage ditch, protecting our right flank pretty effectively with rifles, machine-gun fire, and grenades. Two of Jaynes's men, Specialists Mike Tuszl and Frank Tealer, were wounded, though not seriously. The wounded 4th Platoon grunts, along with four wounded from the cavalry platoon, crawled in the drainage ditch back toward the village.

We need reinforcements, I thought, as I radioed the battalion commander.

"Warrior Six, this is Marauder Six. We need reinforcement. Over," I shouted into the handset.

"Roger. We're working on it. There's a company from the 2d of the 3d Infantry about five clicks to your north moving in your direction. Be advised that your platoon at the POW compound is also in contact. Things are busting loose all over. Over," Mastoris replied.

"Roger. We need gunships, too. Over," I added.

"They're on the way. Over."

"Roger. I'm going to try to evacuate some of my wounded, if I can get an LZ set up. Over."

I had no idea where Holmes was at that moment, so I called him on the radio; I needed him to take charge of the medevac.

"Marauder Five, this is Marauder Six. Where the hell are you? Over," I shouted into the handset.

Holmes was back up the road about seventy-five meters, gathering up the wounded and trying to get the ACAVs out of the mess they were in.

"I've got most of the wounded and some of 3d Platoon with me. I think I'm about a hundred meters to your rear. Over," Holmes responded.

"Roger. See if you can set up an LZ up on Highway 1 for a dust-off," I instructed him. "I've got some gunships en route. I'm staying put until they get here. I'm not sure where the rest of 3d and 4th platoons are. The lead track is knocked out and another is badly damaged. Over," I continued.

"Roger," Holmes responded. "I'm calling for a dust-off. Out!"

I grabbed my two radio operators and an M60 machine gunner who lay nearby and ran toward the door of the house. As we took cover inside the one-room structure, I ordered the M60 gunner to hose down the area behind the house through a rear window. Then I tried to make contact with a pair of gunships I heard circling the area.

From the doorway I had a pretty good view of the road to our front. The knocked-out track was burning well now, and ammunition in the troop compartment was starting to cook off.

Suddenly, my radio came to life, and the lead pilot of the gunship flight came up on my company frequency.

"Marauder Six, this is Knight Twelve. Can you mark your position? Over."

"Roger. Do you see the burning track on the road?"

"Got it, Marauder Six."

"I don't have anyone north of that position. If you make your passes on an east-west axis north of that burning track, you won't hit any friendlies. Over."

"Roger. Got it. We're rolling; keep your heads down. Out."

I didn't realize that Schneider and part of his squad were still up on line with the burning track, preparing to pull back as the gunships rolled in. As the squad hastily withdrew, they were hit with shell casings from the gunships' machine guns. The squad sprinted past the house I was in and headed for the company's new position near Highway 1.

As I directed the gunship strikes, Holmes tried to bring in a medevac helicopter to a small landing zone (LZ) he had set up in a schoolyard. The medevac helicopter, call sign Dust-off

Nineteen, was drawing fire from a VC antiaircraft machine gun on the roof of a hospital in Ho Nai. The dust-off was twice driven off by the enemy fire, but the pilot managed to land in the schoolyard on the third attempt after sustaining multiple hits from the enemy machine gun. The dust-off pilot was awarded the Silver Star for this evacuation under fire.

Holmes loaded ten of the most-seriously wounded Charlie Company and armored cavalry troopers onto the chopper before it lifted off en route to the 93d Evacuation Hospital at Long Binh. Four of the less-seriously wounded chose to stay and fight. The time was now 0530, more than three hours since the first enemy rockets had been fired into the Bien Hoa Air Base.

After Holmes determined that I was still in my forward position and probably cut off, he led a squad from 3d Platoon and moved toward my location.

It was now becoming a bit lighter, but we could see no friendly troops. Kaylor was sure that we were the only ones who had not pulled back. Actually, Sergeant Jaynes and part of his platoon still lay prone along the sides of the ditch on the other side of the road. Sporadic enemy fire tore chunks out of the house's cinder-block walls.

As I peered out the doorway to spot targets for the gunships, I heard Holmes hollering at me from his position about twenty meters up the road.

"You've got to fall back! The company's back up the road. We'll provide covering fire!"

"We're making a break for it," I said to my RTOs and machine gunner. "Stay low!"

We sprinted out the door and through a garden beside the house as Holmes and his squad provided covering fire. We all made it.

Jaynes saw us withdraw and began pulling back up the ditch as we ran for cover.

Another team of gunships came on station and continued to pound the enemy positions as dawn broke over the smoke-covered battlefield.

I knew I had fewer than thirty men left who could fight, and several had painful shrapnel wounds. Six of the seven ACAVs made it back to the village, but one of these was badly damaged.

We set up a perimeter at the road junction. The 106mm recoilless rifle track aimed its gun down the road, and the other ACAVs assumed a herringbone formation along Highway 1.

I radioed the battalion commander and briefed him on my situation. It was now almost 0600.

"This is Marauder Six. What's the status on our reinforcements?" I asked.

"This is Warrior Six. The company from 2/3d is on the high ground about two clicks to your north, digging in," Mastoris replied.

"Why are they digging in? Are they in contact? Over."

"That's a negative. Their Charlie Oscar refused to move south until he's reinforced, so I've requested a mech battalion from the 9th Infantry Division to reinforce you. They're fighting their way up Highway 316 headed toward your location."

"What's the status on Charlie One at the POW compound? Can you release them back to me?" It was a long shot.

"That's a negative, Marauder Six. They're taking heavy automatic fire and have four wounded. The 11th ACR is on the way to reinforce them. Over."

"Roger. Out," I said, ending the transmission.

As I tried to assess our situation, I peered northward through the haze and smoke up the road toward the smoldering hull of the knocked-out ACAV. The gunships were still pummeling the VC. We have to make an attack, I decided; there's no way we can sit here for two hours and let those bastards regroup and reorganize. I thought that we had hurt them badly in the initial contact, but the gunships told me that at least a company of VC was dug in around the cemetery. Maybe more were on the way, I thought.

The Charlie Company attack was set to jump off at 0615. I decided to attack north again, using the road as our axis of advance, but this time the ACAVs would stay behind to secure our rear and protect the road junction. I hated to lose their firepower, but the road was too narrow for them to maneuver. If we made it across the culvert and gained a foothold on the high ground on the other side, I would call the ACAVs forward.

I had the cavalry's 106mm recoilless rifle fire two flechette rounds north, up the road, as we started our attack. The 106 let loose with an angry *boom, boom,* and a blast of thousands of dart-shaped nails tore up the ground ahead.

With 3d Platoon once again off the left side of the road and 4th Platoon on the right, we moved forward and made good progress for the first two hundred meters.

As we approached the burned-out ACAV, an enemy 60mm mortar opened fire from the high ground to our front. I spotted the enemy mortar crew dropping rounds into their tube on the ridgeline. Fortunately, their rounds landed short in the streambed to our front.

I was lying beside Sergeant Jaynes of Charlie Four when I said, "Take those guys out with your M79s."

Seconds later, Jaynes's M79, grenadiers all experts at high-trajectory fire, lobbed round after round of 40mm grenades at the mortar position. They quickly silenced the mortar. One of the VC mortar crewmen took off, deserting his mortar. He didn't get far; a 40mm round already in the air plunged earthward and struck the unlucky VC on the top of the head, killing him instantly.

As we prepared to move forward again, an enemy squad on the west side of the road opened fire with a light machine gun and AK-47s on Wyers's advancing platoon. Wyers's men were pinned down.

Privates first class Alfred Lewis from Detroit, Michigan, and Mike Raugh, a twenty-year-old New Yorker, were crouched in the ditch beside the road when the machine gun opened up. Lewis, who had been under fire before, told Raugh, a new replacement, to stay put, and then he began to crawl forward to have a look. Lewis crept out of the ditch and up a gentle slope until he was silhouetted. The enemy machine gun fired another burst that was quickly answered by a fusillade from 3d Platoon riflemen. Lewis, caught in the crossfire between his own platoon and the enemy, was shot in the head and died instantly.

Third Platoon crawled forward past their dead comrade and engaged the enemy squad. In a brisk firefight they killed eight enemy and captured a light machine gun and an automatic rifle before they were again pinned down by enemy fire from the high ground across the stream. Specialist Byrd, a stalwart Tennesseean, took a round through his cheek that shattered his jaw and knocked out several teeth before it exited. He was medevaced and, despite a heavy loss of blood, survived.

While 3d Platoon mopped up the enemy squad, 4th Platoon and the CP group also had problems. A seemingly fearless enemy soldier armed with a machine pistol suddenly jumped out of the brush and fired a burst that barely missed us. Then he ran for the cover of the culvert, entering it from the right side of the road. We were about fifteen meters from the culvert.

"I think I can take him out with a grenade," my FO shouted.

"OK, but be careful," I yelled back at him.

The FO ran forward, grenade in hand, and made an underhand throw toward the mouth of the steel culvert, then dove into dirt. He missed the opening by inches, and the grenade lay cooking off beside the opening. Assuming the grenade was a dud, the FO raised his body up to the push-up position to have a look. Just then the fragmentation grenade exploded. The FO took a tiny shard of shrapnel in the shoulder; it wasn't life-threatening, but it was bad enough to require medevac.

Meanwhile, the elusive VC crawled through the culvert and emerged on the other side of the road. As we took cover behind the knocked-out ACAV, we saw him at about the same time he saw us. He sprinted toward the vine-covered embankment beside the road and fired a long burst from his machine pistol as he dove into the brush. His burst of 9mm bullets ricocheted off the hull of the burnt ACAV, narrowly missing me, Kaylor, and Sergeant Larry Abel. We opened fire into the embankment and followed up with hand grenades. The first grenade detonated and blew half of the VC's torso out of the brush. Then a second grenade exploded, and the remainder of the body was blown from the brush. It wasn't a pretty sight.

The close and furious combat continued. The VC who dug in at the cemetery poured it on us every time our gunship support departed to rearm and refuel. I was pretty sure that we had mopped up all the pockets of resistance south of the streambed, but there was no way that we could carry the high ground across the stream without reinforcements. I decided to pull the two platoons back about fifty meters and wait for help to arrive.

From our new position, I could still direct the gunship strikes on the area around the cemetery. After another strike, a single VC crawled from his fighting position near the cemetery and ran down the road in our direction, waving his hands in the air above his head. On he came toward our lines in a sprint. I fully expected that one of my soldiers or his own comrades would cut him down. Charlie Company held its fire, and two riflemen jumped onto the road and tackled the VC as he entered our lines. He took a pretty good pummeling from the pissed-off grunts before I could call them off. We had our first prisoner of the battle.

The prisoner, who had only minor shrapnel wounds, was begging my men not to shoot him. I could tell that much, but I couldn't understand what else he was trying to say. My Vietnamese interpreter, Trung, had gone on leave for Tet, and none of us spoke Vietnamese. I thought he might be an officer, but wasn't sure.

"Get him back to the rear; turn him over to Top!" I ordered one of the riflemen. "And make sure he gets there alive; he's trying to tell us something."

As Charlie Company fought its early morning battle, a relief column from the 2d Battalion, 47th Mechanized Infantry, sped north toward Ho Nai. Under the command of Maj. Bill Jones, the battalion operations officer, the column included Alpha Company and elements of Headquarters Company.

When the 2/47th task force received the call to move to Ho Nai, they had been more than twelve kilometers away in a night laager position off Highway 15 southeast of Long Binh. On the road by 0550, the 2/47th M113s barreled down Highway 15 until they reached Highway 316. They then turned north on Highway 316, the major highway connecting Saigon and Long Binh, taking small-arms fire as they made the turn. The column pushed northward along the highway. By 0650, the column was moving past "Widows Village," opposite the II Field Force compound, when they were again fired upon. The 2/47th task force pressed on toward the intersection of Highway 1, where they

turned east into Ho Nai village, again taking fire from small
groups of VC holed up in the village. Jones's armored column fought its way eastward down the highway, bypassing
the enemy resistance.

Specialist Russ Vibberts of the battalion's scout platoon
was driving the lead M113 with Major Jones in the commander's cupola. Following closely behind the major's
track in column formation were Alpha Company's eleven
M113s. When Vibberts realized that his column was taking
fire from the rear, he sped up. When he saw a tall first sergeant standing on the road trying to wave him down, he
barreled past him without stopping. Cursing, First Sergeant
Holmes jumped out of the way to avoid being run over. The
mech column continued down Highway 1 for another kilometer before realizing that they had missed their turnoff.

The 2/47th column had to halt and reverse direction,
speeding back to Holmes's position at the road junction. It
was 0845 by the time Major Jones's task force reached our
location on the dirt road just north of Ho Nai.

I ran to the major's track and briefed him. "Major, glad
you guys made it. I'm CO of Charlie 4/12th Infantry. We've
been in heavy contact since last night. I'm running short on
men, and we need to get across that streambed and take the
high ground on the other side."

"How many VC are dug in on that ridgeline?" Jones
asked.

"Hard to tell, but I'd guess the better part of a company.
The gunships and artillery worked them over pretty good,
but the survivors are putting up one hell of a fight."

I pointed out the enemy positions on the high ground
around the cemetery to Jones, and we hastily developed our
plan of attack.

First, we had to move our infantry across the stream and
gain a foothold above the embankment on the other side.
Then Major Jones could move his M113s across the culvert

and support the advancing infantry in a final assault on the enemy dug in along the ridgeline and in the cemetery.

Jones ordered me to attack with my two Charlie Company platoons on the west (left) side of the road while his dismounted mech troopers from Company A attacked on the east (right) side of the road. Once we gained a foothold on the high ground, Jones would cross the culvert with his tracks and join us.

Moments later we launched the attack as gunships suppressed the enemy fire. My command group, which included Holmes, Kaylor, Abel, the limping Archibald, and me, followed about ten meters behind the assaulting platoons and about twenty meters off the left shoulder of the road. We scrambled down one bank of the streambed and up the other. When I first looked down the streambed, I saw more than a dozen enemy bodies strewn about in the low ground.

Suddenly, a shot rang out behind us. A VC hidden in a cluster of dense vegetation near the culvert was firing at the command group. We were easily identified by the whip antennas protruding from our PRC-25 radios. Kaylor, an expert with the M16, spotted the concealed VC first and fired into the undergrowth to our right rear. Top followed up with a shotgun blast while I fired a burst from my CAR15. The dead VC, riddled with bullet holes, rolled out of the brush.

I glanced to my right to see if Charlie and Alpha were still on line. The mech infantry grunts were already on the edge of the cemetery, pushing on almost too quickly.

The remnants of a battalion of the 275th VC Regiment were dug in on both sides of the road along the military crest of the ridgeline with a strongpoint in the cemetery. Although they had been severely shot up by the circling gunships since before dawn, they still had some fight in them. Although many had fled north to fight again another day

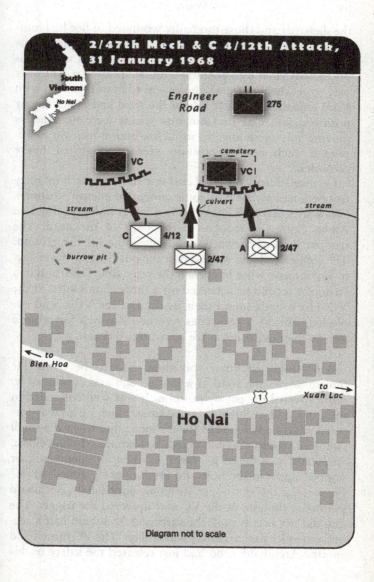

2/47th Mech & C 4/12th Attack, 31 January 1968

South Vietnam

Ho Nai

Engineer Road

275

cemetery

VC

VC

culvert

stream

stream

burrow pit

C 4/12

2/47

A 2/47

to Bien Hoa

to Xuan Loc

1

Ho Nai

Diagram not to scale

the diehards and those too badly wounded to flee had hunkered down in their open fighting positions. Their positions were hard to spot in the weeds and brush, and it was possible to walk right by a position without spotting it. The only way to get them out of the holes was to blast them out with hand grenades. The left side of the road had fewer enemy positions, but Charlie Company grunts were nonetheless moving very methodically, using fire-and-movement to approach each enemy position close enough to heave grenades.

I glanced across the road and saw that the mech infantry troopers had swept past some concealed enemy positions. Suddenly, I saw a VC stand up in a spider hole and shoot an Alpha Company trooper in the back of the head. The trooper lurched forward, dead before he hit the ground. The soldier had just walked past the position; he never saw it. Kaylor saw what happened the same time I did, and in a flash of a second he squeezed off a three-round burst at the VC. His rounds found their mark, and the VC's head exploded. The VC's comrades returned Kaylor's fire from a nearby dugout position. We were pinned down.

Bob Archibald knew something had to be done. He limped across the road in a low crouch and continued to move toward the enemy position. It was well concealed in the grass, and Archibald was cautiously inching his way forward when he saw one of Jones's men point toward a small clump of bushes that concealed the foxhole. Moving closer, Archibald was taken by surprise when an enemy soldier popped up from the hole and fired a poorly aimed AK-47 burst at the 2/47th trooper. Reacting immediately, Archibald pointed a shotgun at the VC and squeezed the trigger. The gun did not fire. It took the surprised Archibald half a second to realize that his safety was still on. The VC turned and spotted Archibald, who had just released the safety on his weapon. Archibald fired a blast, but his aim was low and the pellets spattered into the dirt in front of the VC's hole. The VC ducked back down into the hole while Archibald looked for some cover. He ducked behind a stone pillar at the gateway to the cemetery to reload his shotgun. Next, Archibald slipped cautiously around the pillar to have a look. At that moment, the diehard VC rose up from his hole looking for his target. He spotted Archibald and cut loose with a burst from his AK-47. Archibald returned fire with a shotgun blast as he retreated back to the pillar. He felt a searing heat in his left leg. An AK round had grazed the flesh, leaving a small trickle of blood.

Frustrated with his poor aim with the shotgun, Archibald reached for a grenade. When he remembered that he had thrown all his frags earlier that morning, he looked across the road for help. "I need some frags!" he shouted to us.

First Sergeant Holmes gathered grenades from the command group and nearby grunts. He tossed the unarmed frags across the road to some 2/47th grunts who lay in the ditch beside the road. The grunts then tossed the grenades to Archibald, who was kneeling behind the pillar. Archibald pulled the pin on the first grenade and lobbed it toward the enemy position. The grenade landed square in the enemy foxhole, a perfect throw. Prepared to charge the hole as soon as the grenade detonated, Archibald was shocked when he saw the grenade coming back at him, then detonating in an air burst.

Archibald reached for another grenade, this time remembering his training. He pulled the pin, released the spoon, and counted off two seconds before he threw the grenade. He made another perfect throw, and this time the grenade exploded inside the enemy foxhole. Before the dust settled, Archibald charged the position and emptied his shotgun down into the hole. Four enemy bodies were later pulled from the position. Before the fight was over that day, the wiry twenty-one-year-old from Sunnyvale, California, was personally credited with a total of twelve kills while knocking out three more VC positions. Bob Archibald was awarded the Distinguished Service Cross for his extraordinary heroism during this battle.

Observing that Charlie Company and his own mech company troopers had gained the high ground, Major Jones brought his M113s forward across the culvert and up the hill. The tracks fanned out on the high ground and continued to support the advance with their machine guns. Jones called me over to his command track, and I pointed out a couple of positions that were still holding out. He ordered his M113s forward, and the lumbering fighting vehicles rolled over the foxholes, their wide tracks crushing the enemy soldiers.

Alpha and Charlie soldiers began escorting small groups of enemy prisoners back down the road toward our location. There were thirteen in all, most of whom were wounded. A couple of the prisoners told Major Jones's interpreter that they were NVA replacements. More than fifty enemy bodies were strewn along the ridgeline, most near the VC strongpoint in the cemetery. A total of three U.S. soldiers died in the fighting to seize the ridgeline and cemetery, and several more were wounded.

Major Jones told me and his Alpha Company commander to continue the attack northward along both sides of the road until we linked up with the 2/3d Infantry company dug in on a hilltop about a kilometer to our north.

Although we were exhausted by the heavy fighting, we pushed northward and met light resistance. A few minutes after 1400, we reached the Company B, 2/3d perimeter. The "Old Guard" company commander's first words to me were that one of his men had been killed by friendly fire.

"What?" I asked incredulously. "Do you realize what's

been going on for the past ten hours while you were sitting on your asses on this hill? Why didn't you try to link up with us last night instead of digging in? We were fighting an enemy battalion less than a click down the road." I continued to point south down the road. "If one of your men was shot, it was the VC that got him, not us!" I said angrily.

The battalion commander of the 2/3d relieved the captain later that day. Our acting brigade commander, Col. Davison, had closely monitored the battle and had little patience for timidity in his commanders.

I radioed Major Jones that we had linked up with the Old Guard company, and he told me to pull back to his location. When we arrived, Jones said he had received a new mission order: Move to Bien Hoa and join the fight for the air base. I was sorry to see Major Jones and his 2/47th troopers depart our area. The bold mech infantrymen loaded onto their M113s and rolled off toward Bien Hoa.

What's next, I wondered as I reached for my radio. Lieutenant Colonel Mastoris ordered me to dig in facing north along the edge of the village. We were going to be attached to the 2/3d Infantry, and their commander, Lt. Col. Bill Carper, was on his way with further instructions. Bravo Company, 2/3d, was ordered south from its hilltop position to join us. Carper flew in by Huey to our location. The colonel walked around, looking at some of the enemy dead, and told his own commander and me to start digging in on the same terrain we had fought for the previous night. Before flying back to his headquarters, he told us that he had another rifle company on the way to reinforce us.

We dug our positions on the east side of the road as darkness enveloped us. Shortly after dark, Charlie Company, 2/3d, arrived to extend our perimeter to the east. Carper had warned us that two battalions of the 275th were still in the vicinity, so we expected a night attack.

At 2330 we spotted a small VC patrol to our front and

engaged it with M79 grenade fire, killing two. The nervous 2/3d Infantry commanders called artillery fire missions forward of their positions all night. I fell into a deep sleep shortly after midnight.

1–2 February

As I woke in the dewy grass beside the hole that Top Holmes and I had dug the evening before, I glanced around to see if my radio operators were alert. Kaylor was on radio watch, sitting beside his foxhole with his M16 on his lap, munching down some C ration crackers smeared with cheese.

"Kaylor, that cheese'll kill you," I grumbled.

"Better than a head shot."

"Where's Top?" I asked.

"Checking the perimeter. Sergeant Jaynes said there's two dead VC in front of his platoon's position. His guys got 'em with M79s last night."

I walked to a nearby bush to urinate. It was warm for early morning, and the air was fouled with the stench of unburied bodies.

Holmes returned to the CP a few minutes later. "Jaynes got two more last night, Captain," Holmes reported.

"How's Wyers's platoon holding up?"

"Wyers said a couple of villagers came to his CP this morning. They were carrying a message from their priest. He wants us to provide security for a burial party for some civilians who were killed by the VC yesterday. They said the VC were hiding in their village for a week." Ho Nai village was populated primarily by Catholic Vietnamese, who had left North Vietnam after the French-Indochina War.

"Send some troops from 3d Platoon. Doesn't look like much is going to happen today."

My prediction was only partly right. That morning we were ordered to search the houses in Ho Nai. We took two wounded VC prisoner. The villagers were mad as hell at the VC and wanted us to turn these prisoners over to them, promising us speedy justice. They also asked us for weapons. I turned down both requests.

I got some good news shortly after noon. My 1st Platoon, still at the POW compound, would be released from that mission later in the day. They were to move to our location at Ho Nai along with a platoon from D Troop, 17th Cavalry.

Tuber's 1st Platoon, reinforced by a platoon from D/17th Cavalry, had beaten off a company-size night attack on the POW compound while we battled the enemy at Ho Nai. Twenty-six enemy soldiers fell while attempting to liberate their comrades inside the compound. Not a single enemy soldier managed to breach the barbed-wire fence that enclosed the camp.

Late in the afternoon of 1 February, the 2/3d battalion commander returned to our location and briefed me and his two company commanders on the mission for that night. I didn't like what he had to say.

Lieutenant Colonel Carper ordered me to move Charlie Company north to the hilltop on which his own Bravo Company had loitered on the night of 31 January. Bravo and Charlie companies of his battalion would continue to defend the village. He also told us that, even though the VC had been badly mauled over the past thirty-six hours, there was still an enemy battalion unaccounted for in the fighting so far.

"The battalion belongs to the 275th Regiment, and according to the intelligence, there's a good chance they'll be moving west through our area tonight, toward Bien Hoa."

"If that VC battalion hits my night defensive position on that hill, I may need some help. Those odds are a bit steep, Sir."

"I can reinforce you from the village if need be. You're

getting your 1st Platoon back along with another cav platoon. Dig in good, and you should be able to hold that high ground, Captain."

"Roger, Sir." I was apprehensive about my mission.

Why didn't the 2/3d commander order one of his own full-strength companies to defend the hill? Even with Tuber's platoon, I was still short a rifle platoon. I had also lost the equivalent of half a platoon in the first two days of fighting. Nonetheless, I knew that colonels didn't usually explain the rationale for the orders they gave.

We trudged northward in a double column up the now familiar dirt road and reached the highest elevation on the hill shortly after 1800. The jungle had been bulldozed back about seventy-five meters from the road that bisected the hill. The road continued north off the hill and down a long finger toward the Dong Nai River. We set up a 360-degree perimeter along the military crest of the hill and interspersed the ACAVs among my two rifle platoons. The rocky ground made it tough to dig fighting positions more than a foot or two deep. The weary grunts used their meager supply of sandbags to construct firing parapets around their positions and then wolfed down a supper of cold C rations.

I was worried about fire support. Thus far, we had trouble getting artillery fire missions. There were simply too many fire missions for the artillery to accomplish. I needed my own 81mm mortars to defend the hill. Firing from our NDP, the mortarmen could lay down a barrage directly on the edge of our perimeter. There was no lag time. We had practiced this type of defensive fire.

I radioed Mastoris at FSB Concord to request that the mortars be flown in immediately.

"I need those three 81s to defend this position," Mastoris said.

"Keep two tubes at Concord, and send me one," I counter-offered.

"Okay, you've got one tube, and all the ammo I can load on one supply bird," Mastoris replied.

I gave Jaynes a heads-up and told him to start plotting defensive fires around the perimeter. The mortar men were elated. Because my FO had been dusted off the day before, I plotted my own artillery DEFCONs. Recalling his night on Old Baldy during the Korean War, Holmes advised me to "ring the hill with steel."

A UH-1 landed inside our perimeter twenty minutes later with one 81mm mortar and sixty rounds of high-explosive ammunition. Jaynes's men unloaded the mortar and ammo from the Huey and had the mortar set up five minutes later. I felt more confident with that 81mm mortar in our NDP.

Just before dark, 1st Platoon rolled into the perimeter with five ACAVs from D/17th Cavalry. My confidence shot up another notch. If attacked, we now had a fighting chance with three platoons of infantry and two platoons of cavalry. I briefed Lieutenant Tuber and gave him a sector of the perimeter to defend.

Twilight came and went while I positioned Tuber's men in the perimeter. By the time I returned to my CP, the hill was shrouded in darkness. My gut feeling was that we would be attacked before the night was over. I wasn't wrong.

Shortly after 2030, we spotted a group of VC as it crossed the road about 150 meters north of the perimeter. Almost simultaneously, enemy automatic weapons fire came from the south and west. I radioed Jaynes and told him to put mortar fire on the VC to the north. Then I called for artillery and gunship support to eliminate the enemy fire from the south and west.

The DEFCONs that I had plotted to the west of the

perimeter were too far off to silence the enemy fire; I had to make bold adjustments to get the rounds on target. Meanwhile, Jaynes's mortar fire, along with some M79 and .50-caliber machine gun fire, broke up the VC attack on the north side. However, Jaynes was running low on mortar ammo.

A few minutes later, a gunship team was on station, followed shortly by an Air Force AC-47 "Spooky" flare ship. Flying in a high orbit over the rocky hill, the AC-47 illuminated the area with bright magnesium flares. I radioed my platoon leaders to mark their locations with strobe lights, then I began to direct the gunship strikes on the enemy.

The helicopter gunships pounded the VC on the west side of the perimeter with machine guns and rockets. Spooky's minigun hosed down the VC to our east with undulating streams of glowing red tracers. The staccato bursts from the gunships' 7.62mm machine guns were punctuated by the buzz-saw sound of the AC-47's minigun.

We continued to receive small-arms fire for the next hour or so as the enemy probed our perimeter looking for a weak spot. Spooky and the gunships continued shooting at anything that moved outside the perimeter.

At 2335 the battle began to intensify along the east side of the perimeter. An RPG barrage slammed into the perimeter, scoring a direct hit on an ACAV and seriously wounding six members of the crew. Spooky shifted its fire to target the undergrowth just beyond our perimeter. Its blazing minigun started several small fires in the brush.

Because Spooky and the gunships were suppressing the VC fire, I decided to call a dust-off for the six seriously wounded troopers. The medevac helicopter arrived a few minutes before midnight and attempted to land on the southern side of our perimeter, where the incoming fire was weakest. On the first try, the pilot was driven off by a barrage of enemy fire. After the gunships shifted their fire, the dust-off pilot made another approach, this time touching down outside the perimeter.

I radioed the pilot. "Dust-off Nineteen, Dust-off Nineteen, you're outside the perimeter. Repeat, you're outside the perimeter in an unsecured area."

"Roger. I'm lifting off. Mark a landing site inside the perimeter with a strobe. Over."

I shouted at a soldier near my location, tossed him my strobe light, and told him to mark a spot for the dust-off to land.

On the next attempt, the dust-off landed inside the perimeter under heavy fire that wounded the soldier with the strobe. Only four wounded made it onto the medevac before the pilot had to lift off under intense fire. The dust-off sustained several hits but evaded more by flying low over the trees until he cleared the battle area.

The battle continued unabated. I was still worried about a ground attack on the eastern side of the perimeter. I radioed the battalion commander of the 2/3d Infantry to request reinforcement and resupply. We were burning up ammo quickly; I was concerned about running out.

"Can you hold out until first light?" Carper asked.

"This is Marauder Six. I don't know. My ammo is limited. Over."

"Roger. I'll send you reinforcements. Over."

Shortly after this radio conversation, a U.S. Air Force forward air controller (FAC) orbiting overhead in his spotter aircraft came up on my radio frequency and asked if I needed close air support (CAS). It was now after 0100.

"This is Marauder Six. That's affirmative. Do you have any birds in the air? Over."

"This is Drama Nineteen. I have two VNAF [Vietnamese Air Force] fighters one minute out."

"This is Marauder Six. What type of ordnance do they have?"

C 4/12th Night Defense, 1–2 February 1968

South Vietnam

Ho Nai

Engineer Road

automatic-weapons fire

4C

RPG fire

C   4/12

3C

1C

machine-gun fire

main VC attack

to Ho Nai

●●●   Infantry platoon deployment

ACAV track

VC fire

Diagram not to scale

"This is Drama Nineteen. They're returning from another strike and only have rockets."

I had no experience with and little confidence in the VNAF pilots, particularly at night. Moreover, I knew that rockets were sometimes erratic in flight, and could do more damage to us than the enemy. It wasn't worth the risk.

"This is Marauder Six. That's a negative on the VNAF strike. I need napalm and cannon fire on the east side of my perimeter. Over."

"This is Drama Nineteen. Roger. I can scramble a flight of U.S. out of Bien Hoa, if you can hang on for two zero minutes. Over."

"This is Marauder Six. Roger. We'll wait. Out."

A pair of U.S. Air Force F-4s were on station at 0130. I coordinated with the FAC to have the jets strike the enemy positions in the dense jungle a hundred meters east of the perimeter using a south-to-north approach.

Seconds later, the Phantoms screamed in at treetop level and dropped their napalm canisters. We could feel the blast of heat as the napalm ignited, and troops on the eastern side of the perimeter reported seeing VC run out of the tree line on fire and screaming. Leaving nothing to chance, the Phantoms struck the same area again, this time using their 20mm cannon. The airstrike broke the backbone of the enemy assault, although the perimeter continued to take sporadic fire.

In the burning firelight from the jungle and the overhead flares, we could now see the point element of the relief force from Company C, 2/3d Infantry, approaching our perimeter from the south. Ten additional ACAVs accompanied the column. Gunships covered both flanks of the relief column with an awesome display of firepower. The column took only sporadic fire from the demoralized enemy and suffered only two casualties in the link-up operation. As the column entered our perimeter, I knew the battle was over at last. We called in

another dust-off to evacuate more wounded, then redistrib-
uted a supply of ammo delivered by the relief column. The
remainder of the night was quiet, with only occasional artillery flares illuminating the area around our perimeter.

As the faint light of dawn appeared over the horizon, I
surveyed the scene. Smoke from the burning jungle and the
gutted ACAV hung low over the hillock. The air was con-
taminated with the smell of cordite, napalm, and burnt human flesh. Moments later, three dazed and terribly burned
VC wandered into the perimeter.

I sent out a patrol to the battered jungle to the east, and
they radioed back that they had found more than fifty bodies burned beyond recognition. I walked around the
perimeter and talked with some of my men. I saw that their
eyes were bloodshot and three days' growth of beard covered their weary young faces. A few wandered outside the
perimeter to claim the weapons laying beside enemy
corpses. Almost every member of Charlie Company now
carried a captured AK-47 in addition to his own M16 rifle.

Nowhere had the VC actually breached the perimeter, although some made it to within twenty-five yards of our positions. The gunships and CAS had broken up the attack.

We spent the morning redistributing ammunition and
sent patrols into the jungle. We found more weapons and
bodies and took one additional prisoner.

Charlie Company was released from operational control of
the 2/3d Infantry at 1335, and we were ordered to return to
FSB Concord. We mounted the ACAVs and rumbled off the
battle-scarred hilltop en route to Concord. Feeling physically
and emotionally drained, I lit a cigarette and inhaled deeply.

The ACAVs rolled into Concord thirty minutes later.
Lieutenant Colonel Mastoris and Sergeant Major Moon
met us. As the exhausted Charlie Company warriors dismounted the tracks, I followed the battalion commander to
his bunker for a debriefing.

After I had summarized Charlie Company's actions over the past seventy-two hours, Mastoris informed me that Charlie Company was credited with decimating a battalion of the 275th VC Regiment. That regiment was assigned to the 5th VC Division. The battalion we had defeated was part of a regiment-size attack on the Long Binh complex. He also mentioned that prisoners we had taken confirmed that the 88th NVA Regiment had provided fillers to bring their battalion up to strength before the attack.

Continuing, Mastoris informed me that the Communists still held portions of the Cholon section of Saigon, and major fighting continued in Hue, Kontum, Pleiku, Dalat, and the suburbs of many other towns and cities from the Mekong Delta to the DMZ. He also said that Charlie Company could be deployed again at a moment's notice. I struggled to focus on what he was saying as the cold beer he had opened for me began to dull my senses.

chapter six

night airmobile assault

The final test of a leader is that he leaves behind him in
other men the conviction and the will to carry on.
—WALTER LIPPMANN,
New York Herald Tribune

Night Airmobile Assault

We had only a day's rest at FSB Concord after the battle at
Ho Nai. Charlie Company still was on call as the brigade
ready-reaction force, and a new mission was not long in coming. Shortly after 1700 on 3 February, I was told to report to
the TOC for a briefing. The S-3, Maj. Ed King, informed me
that an intelligence source had reported the location of the
5th VC Division Headquarters. He pointed to a location on
the situation map about twenty clicks east of Concord. The
brigade commander wanted Charlie Company to air assault
into the area and locate the VC headquarters. The 5th VC Division had coordinated and controlled the Tet attacks against
Bien Hoa and Long Binh. Although King did not reveal the
intelligence source, I figured that it was based on radio inter-
cepts. These reports were rated as "highly reliable." Nonetheless, I figured the VC were probably already on the move;
they had good communications discipline and rarely stayed
put after transmitting radio messages.

King also told me that a brigade LRRP was already on the
ground in the same vicinity and had reported some enemy
sightings. I asked the S-2 about the strength of the 5th VC Division Headquarters and its security force. He didn't know.

I told King that my men were still exhausted from the previous fighting and needed more rest. He was unmoved. Charlie Company was still the brigade ready-reaction force, and this was a brigade-directed mission.

Then I asked if Charlie Company still had the mission of defending Concord. The answer was yes. This meant that Charlie Company had only two rifle platoons available for the airmobile assault. Mortar Platoon and one rifle platoon would have to remain behind to defend Concord.

Although I didn't like the mission, I understood that we were the only company available. In Saigon the 3/7th Infantry was still fighting it out with the diehard VC in the Cholon section, and we were receiving warnings of a second wave of attacks yet to come during February. Few doubted the enemy's intent to continue their nationwide offensive.

The 5th VC Division was reeling from the relentless U.S. counterattacks. Its 275th VC Regiment was decimated at Ho Nai and Long Binh, and the 274th VC Regiment was badly mauled at Bien Hoa. However, at least one NVA regiment was supposed to be in southern War Zone D. The 88th NVA Regiment, normally reported around Pleiku in the Central Highlands, had apparently moved south to support the VC divisions for the Tet Offensive. The 88th had provided manpower support to the 5th VC Division's regiments prior to their attacks, but no one knew what they were up to now. An NVA regiment unaccounted for in our area made me even more apprehensive.

After briefing my platoon leaders, the 1st and 3d platoons saddled up and moved to a pick-up zone just outside the berm of the fire base. The troops broke into six-man loads and lined up on both sides of the pick-up zone by 1830. We were going in prepared for the worst, with rucksacks crammed full of extra M16 magazines, grenades, Claymores, and LAWs. Each squad carried double its basic load of 7.62mm M60 ammo.

The men grumbled and clearly were not happy about another mission. Everyone, including me, was worried about a hot landing zone (LZ). A delay in the pick-up time increased our stress level.

As the evening wore on, we were told that all of II Field Force's aviation assets were committed, but that our mission was still on. The 199th Brigade, 101st Airborne, 9th Infantry, 1st Infantry, and 25th Infantry divisions all were in competition for II Field Force aviation support.

By 1900 hours, everyone was hoping that the mission would be scrubbed, and we would get the order to return to the fire base for hot chow and a good night's rest. It was not to be.

I had requested the battalion's C&C ship to recon the LZ, but Mastoris didn't want to tip our hand to the enemy. By now it was apparent that Charlie Company would be making a night airmobile assault, my first. I knew such operations required tight control and coordination, particularly with the fire support from artillery and gunships. Furthermore, I knew that a night insertion was much more confusing for the troops once on the ground.

I briefed my platoon leaders on where they would be landing and assembling on the LZ and ensured that they had strobe lights to mark their positions once we landed. We anticipated a single lift of ten UH-1s. That would be enough lift to put both platoons and the CP group on the LZ at the same time.

As darkness fell, the grunts finished off cans of cold C rations. They bitched because they knew their buddies on the bunker line were enjoying a hot meal prepared by the battalion mess section. The security of our pick-up zone also began to concern me; during the hours of darkness, a large stand of rubber trees bordering the LZ provided excellent concealment for VC.

About 1915 hours, I received a radio message from the

TOC indicating that the only air assets available were the 17th Air Cavalry's UH-1s. These aircraft were normally used to lift the troop's aero-rifle platoon. This lift platoon consisted of only four UH-1s, making three lifts necessary to insert my two rifle platoons and CP group into the LZ. The first lift with twenty-five men would land on a potentially hot LZ in darkness and would have to secure the LZ for at least thirty minutes before the UH-1s returned to insert the second lift. We would then wait another thirty minutes for the third lift. Even with artillery and gunship support, the first troops on the ground might not be able to hold the LZ against a determined enemy force. I decided to take my command group in on the first lift.

As darkness descended, we spotted the slicks inbound toward our pick-up zone. There were four, as promised. I pulled the pin on a smoke grenade and tossed it to the ground to mark the spot where the lead helicopter should touch down.

The men sprinted through swirling clouds of dust to board the Hueys. The side doors and web seats had been removed from the helicopters. We clambered aboard and sat on the floor of the aircraft. Some grunts dangled their legs from the open doors. The faces of the men were impassive as we lifted off into the darkening skies. We could see the howitzers at Concord belching tongues of flame from their barrels as the LZ preparation began. The whine of the Huey's turbine engine muffled the sound of the howitzers. The shells screamed over the berm of the fire base on their way to the remote jungle landing zone.

We climbed over the rubber trees below and banked right, then flew northward over the dark winding ribbon of the Dong Nai River into southern War Zone D. As I peered downward into the darkened landscape, I was startled to see dozens of small campfires shimmering through jungle canopy. This was odd because the NVA and VC usually enforced light discipline at night to avoid detection by surveillance aircraft. Retreating survivors of the Tet attacks on Long Binh, many of whom were wounded, must have lit these fires. They probably needed the comfort of a warm fire and some cooked rice.

As the aircraft banked east, we could see our LZ several kilometers south of the confluence of the Song Be and Dong Nai rivers. Aerial flares hung over the LZ, and flashes from ground artillery bursts indicated that the LZ prep was ongoing. The bursting shells set fire to brush around the LZ. A layer of smoke formed over the ground.

The pilot signaled to me that the LZ was straight ahead. The UH-1 skimmed over the treetops and the door gunners began pumping M60 bursts into the undergrowth at the edge of the clearing. The pilot raised the nose of the aircraft as he committed to a landing. The grunts slid themselves toward the open doors until they could dangle their legs over the sides and brace their jungle boots on the landing skids. I did the same. I felt an adrenaline rush as I stood on the skids. As I looked down between my feet, I saw the treetops swaying from the rotor wash. The ship dropped into the clearing, and I leaped off into the grass before the skids touched the ground.

The other three ships landed behind us in trail formation as the artillery bombardment lifted. Bent double beneath the whirling rotor blades, we ran through tornadolike dust and smoke from the rotor wash and toward the darkened jungle. The *wop-wop-wop* of the aircraft lifting off was deafening. Looking over my shoulder, I saw Lieutenant Tuber's men fanning out across the clearing to secure the LZ. There was no enemy fire. I recalled the Vietnam grunt adage, "Happiness is a cold LZ."

Tuber radioed me to confirm that the LZ was cold. We were now alone, about thirty of us on a dark LZ surrounded by jungle. An occasional artillery flare popped above us, breaking the silence and hanging briefly in the blackened sky before drifting downward on a small white parachute, rocking back and forth to cast oscillating dark shadows around us. As the flare burned out, all became quiet. Only the low-volume static of the radio sets broke the stillness. I checked the luminous dial of my compass to orient my map, then crawled under a poncho with a flashlight to plan our route of march.

As soon as the third lift landed, we would move into the jungle several hundred meters, then change direction to link up with the LRRP. Changing the direction of our line of march would decrease the chances of an enemy ambush.

I crawled over to Kaylor's radio, grabbed the handset, and switched to the LRRP frequency. I got the patrol leader on the radio and told him we were on the ground about a thousand meters away. He said that he had heard our choppers and that he also heard movement and noises near his position. He sounded nervous as he spoke in a low whisper. I told him to hold his position and we would get moving toward his location as soon as all my troops had landed.

We needed to get off the LZ as soon as possible; we had too few men to defend it. Grabbing a Starlight Scope, I peered through the eyepiece. I couldn't detect any movement in the tree line on the luminescent yellow-green lens. Everything was eerily quiet.

Ten minutes later we heard the UH-1s bearing down on our LZ with the second lift. I radioed the flight leader and instructed him to have his door gunners hold their fire on this insertion. I didn't want any of my men already on the ground hit by friendly fire.

The second and third lifts went smoothly, and the slicks lifted off without taking any fire. As the helicopters flew off into the night, a feeling of isolation overtook us. Charlie Company was now on its own, deep in an enemy-controlled area. Our only link to the outside world was the radio that Kaylor carried. Although we hadn't taken any fire, any enemy

within several thousand meters knew where we were. We had
to get off that LZ—the sooner the better.

It was so dark, and the jungle was so thick, that we had
to move in single file, each grunt following within arm's
length of the man in front. Bunching up the men like this
was risky, but spreading out could have led to losing someone in the thick undergrowth. Tangles of vine-covered
trees, creepers, and thorny "wait-a-minute" bushes impeded our movement. The column trudged on at an irritat-
ingly slow pace. Distance is difficult to judge at night,
especially in the jungle. I hoped that we wouldn't encounter
any bamboo thickets. Cutting through bamboo would
make far too much noise. The air was heavy, and the smell
of mold and rotting vegetation penetrated our nostrils. At
the halt, we could hear the noises of insects and small noc-
turnal animals rustling through the underbrush. The night
operation became a surreal nightmare. It was as if we were
moving blindly into a dark primeval gallery. When exposed
to these types of stimuli, one experiences a primal fear of
being the prey. Fight-or-flight messages from the brain
cause the heartbeat to quicken and nerves and muscles to
become taut. Focusing on the mission becomes difficult.

After two hundred meters, I radioed my point squad to
make a 90-degree turn, taking up a heading that would
move us toward the LRRP's position. After another half-
hour of painstakingly slow movement, we heard not far off
to our front the staccato burst of a machine gun. Because
the dense jungle muffled the sound, it was difficult to estimate the distance. The firing ceased after a few seconds.

I halted the column and radioed the LRRP team sergeant
to find out what the hell was going on. He said that his men
had heard voices to their front and opened fire. Damned
stupid, I thought, giving away your position like that, especially with an M60. The patrol should have thrown hand

grenades, or just sat tight. Maybe it was us that they heard. Sound carries a long way at night, even in the jungle.

We trudged on. I began to think that the whole operation was absurd. The enemy could be twenty meters to our left or right and we'd never spot them. They could ambush us, or just let us move on past their position.

We moved about another three hundred meters when the LRRPs opened fire again. Kaylor's radio crackled just then, and the silence of the night was shattered by the LRRP sergeant's voice.

"Marauder Six, this is Bishop Forty-one. Over!" Kaylor turned in my direction and handed me the handset: "Sir, Bishop Forty-one."

"I heard it!" I whispered. "Turn down the goddamn volume on that radio set before every VC within ten miles hears it."

"It's on low volume," Kaylor retorted. "Sound just carries more at night."

I grabbed the handset and answered the radio call. "Bishop Forty-one, this is Marauder Six. What's your situation?"

"We've spotted five VC to our front . . . breaking contact . . . moving to an alternate location."

"This is Marauder Six. Roger. Keep me advised."

When the LRRP sergeant reached his rally point, we moved out again in his direction. After another forty minutes of torturous night movement, I thought we were within a couple of hundred meters of the LRRP's new position. Once again they opened fire, the noise amplified by the night. This time we were close enough to hear the machine-gun rounds ripping through the dense foliage to our front. My men instinctively dropped to the ground. Kaylor took another call on the radio from the patrol leader, who reported hearing voices speaking in Vietnamese near his new hiding place.

By now, I knew there was a high risk of casualties from friendly fire if we continued to move. I radioed the battalion TOC and gave my assessment of the situation to Lieutenant Colonel Mastoris. He asked me if I was close enough to move to the LRRP's assistance if they got into a full-blown firefight. I answered in the affirmative. Mastoris then instructed me to move as close as possible without risking my own men, and then establish link-up at first light. Good enough, I thought.

I radioed my platoon leaders to set up a defensive perimeter in the maze of thickets surrounding us. We didn't dig in because that would have been too noisy. We set up Claymores and trip flares in front of our positions, and that was it.

An eerie silence ensued. I informed the nervous LRRP sergeant of our plans as his team went to ground in their new location.

I studied my map under a poncho, trying to second-guess where the 5th VC Division Headquarters might be located. There was a hill mass to our north, designated Nui Go Giap on my map, that may have given them better radio communications, but I concluded that they were probably on the move by now.

It was looking for a needle in a haystack at night. Maybe the enemy thought that we were a larger force than we really were. What the hell, I thought, might as well try to get some sleep.

I rested my back against my rucksack and dozed off to the sound of mosquitoes buzzing around my ears and the distant thump of artillery harassment and interdiction (H&I) fire. My last moments of consciousness were spent wondering if our position was accurately plotted at the artillery fire direction centers. I slept fitfully and woke up several times.

At around 0500, artillery rounds began impacting in the jungle between our position and the LRRP's location. Some

Troops of the Warrior battalion, 4/12 Infantry, attend religious services in the field. December 1967. Photo by 40th Public Information Detachment, 199th Infantry Brigade.

Warrior commanders, January 1968. From left to right: Capt. Pete Albers, Capt. Bob Reynolds, Capt. Bob Eaton, Lt. Col. Bill Schroeder, Capt. Stan McLaughlin, Capt. Bob Tyson, Capt. Bob Tonsetic. Author's photo.

Spc. Cliff Kaylor, Charlie Company RTO. January 1968. Photo courtesy of Cliff Kaylor.

Army helicopter gunships blast enemy positions north of Ho Nai Village on 31 January 1968. Photo by Specialist Dupuis, 40th Public Information Detachment, 199th Infantry Brigade.

Destroyed ACAV from 3d Platoon, Delta Troop, 17th Armored Cavalry, at Ho Nai Village on 31 January 1968. Photo by 1st Lt. Mike Swearingen, 40th Public Information Detachment, 199th Infantry Brigade.

Weapons and VC dead left in the aftermath of 31 January 1968 attacks on Ho Nai Village. Photo by Capt. R. K. Anderson, 40th Public Information Detachment, 199th Infantry Brigade.

Charlie Company Warriors with .51 caliber machine gun captured near Ho Nai Village on 31 January 1968. From left to right: Spc. Kenneth Barber, Spc. Jerold Partch, Spc. Nick Schneider. Photo by 40th Public Information Detachment, 199th Infantry Brigade.

Col. Frederic Davison (*left*), deputy commander of the 199th Infantry Brigade, conferring with (*left to right*), Lt. Col. Herbert Ray, 5/12 Infantry, and Lt. Col. Bill Mastoris, 4/12 Infantry. At right is 199th Brigade S-3 Lt. Col. Don Bolduc. March 1968. Photo by Capt. R. K. Anderson, 40th Public Information Detachment, 199th Infantry Brigade.

Spc. Jerry Partch of Charlie Company, 4/12 Infantry, during Operation Valley Forge, March 1968. Photo by Pfc. W. C. Hansell, 40th Public Information Detachment, 199th Infantry Brigade.

Brig. Gen. Robert C. Forbes (*center*), 199th Infantry Brigade Commanding General, looks over the base camp of 4/12 Infantry with Lt. Col. Bill Mastoris (*right*), commander of 4/12 Infantry. 1st Lt. Douglas Lee (*left*), the general's aide, accompanies them. 13 April 1968. Photo by Spc. Joe Whinnery, 40th Public Information Detachment, 199th Infantry Brigade.

Pfc. James McKensie of Delta Company, 4/12 Infantry, inspects captured NVA weapons and gear after contact five miles southwest of Saigon. 6 May 1968. Photo by Spc. Joe Whinnery, 40th Public Information Detachment, 199th Infantry Brigade.

CH-47 Chinook helicopter lands supplies at Fire Support Base Stephanie (4/12 Infantry) on 7 May 1968. Author's photo.

Duster in action on northern perimeter of Fire Support Base Stephanie on 7 May 1968. Author's photo.

An NVA Hoi Chanh points out NVA positions in the village of Binh Tri Dong, two miles west of Saigon, on 8 May 1968. Photo by Spc. J. Van Wyngarden, 40th Public Information Detachment, 199th Infantry Brigade.

Using smoke to cover their movements, infantrymen from 4/12 Infantry advance toward enemy positions west of Saigon on 8 May 1968. Photo by Spc. J. Van Wyngarden, 40th Public Information Detachment, 199th Infantry Brigade.

Warriors from 4/12 Infantry advance under fire from NVA west of Saigon on 8 May 1968. Photo by Spc. J. Van Wyngarden, 40th Public Information Detachment, 199th Infantry Brigade.

Two Warriors of 4/12 Infantry hit the dirt while assaulting NVA positions west of Saigon on 8 May 1968. Photo by Spc. J. Van Wyngarden, 40th Public Information Detachment, 199th Infantry Brigade.

ACAV of D Troop, 17th Cavalry, 199th Infantry Brigade, provide covering fire to advancing Warriors of 4/12 Infantry west of Saigon on 8 May 1968. Photo by Spc. J. Van Wyngarden, 40th Public Information Detachment, 199th Infantry Brigade.

Warriors of 4/12 Infantry pause to watch a "Freedom Bird," a plane full of soldiers going home, fly overhead. 8 May 1968. Photo by Spc. J. Van Wyngarden, 40th Public Information Detachment, 199th Infantry Brigade.

U.S. Air Force fighters attack NVA position in Binh Tri Dong, west of Saigon, on 8 May 1968. Photo by Spc. J. Van Wyngarden, 40th Public Information Detachment, 199th Infantry Brigade.

1st Sgt. George Holmes of Charlie Company, 4/12 Infantry, escorts captured NVA soldier to Fire Support Base Stephanie on 7 May 1968. Photo by Spc. Joe Whinnery, 40th Public Information Detachment, 199th Infantry Brigade.

Maj. Ed Kelley of 4/12 Infantry plots enemy positions at Fire Support Base Stephanie Tactical Operations Center during the May 1968 Tet Offensive. Author's photo.

Capt. Bob Tonsetic, Charlie Company Commander, 4/12 Infantry, catches up with the news during the lull in the fighting. May 1968. Author's photo.

1st Sgt. George Holmes, Charlie Company, 4/12 Infantry, inspects the troops at Fire Support Base Stephanie. June 1968. Author's photo.

Spc. Robert Archibald receives the Distinguished Service Cross for his actions during the Tet Offensive of 1968. Gen. Creighton Abrams presents the award at Fire Support Base Stephanie. June 1968. Author's photo.

Lt. Col. William Mastoris, Gen. Creighton Abrams, and Brig. Gen. Frederic Davison at award ceremony for Spc. Robert Archibald at Fire Support Base Stephanie. June 1968. Author's photo.

Warriors of 4/12 Infantry await helicopters to land on pick-up zone near Fire Support Base Stephanie. June 1968. Photo by 40th Public Information Detachment, 199th Infantry Brigade.

Capt. Robert Tonsetic, commander of Charlie Company, 4/12 Infantry, receives the Distinguished Service Cross from Gen. Creighton Abrams, Commanding General, Vietnam, for his actions during the 1968 Tet Offensive. Photo by 221st Signal Company.

Officers of 4/12 Infantry, the Warrior battalion. June 1968. Photo courtesy of Col. Paul Viola.

Chaplin Angelo Litkey (*left*), 199th Infantry Brigade Catholic Chaplin, and Maj. Ed Kelley, 4/12 Infantry, talk with a Warrior infantryman at Fire Support Base Stephanie. June 1968. Photo by 40th Public Information Detachment, 199th Infantry Brigade.

twenty-five to thirty 105mm howitzer rounds shattered the ground to our front. I radioed Brigade for a check fire, wondering who had ordered the fire, and if they knew our location.

By dawn I was anxious to conclude this operation. I radioed the LRRP sergeant and told him we would advance toward their location and gave them our direction of approach.

We found the LRRP about an hour later, well hidden in a small copse of bamboo at the edge of a small clearing. There was no sign of any enemy, but I sent out four small patrols in a cloverleaf pattern to recon the surrounding area. They reported back that they'd found no sign of the enemy.

I radioed Mastoris to update him on our situation and request that we be extracted along with the LRRP. He agreed. The men of Charlie Company were tired and pissed off, but we were all relieved.

We flew back to FSB Concord at 1030. A shower and bath unit had been set up at the fire base. When the Charlie Company troopers spotted the large round water storage tank sitting like an above-ground pool, they dropped their rucks and weapons and raced toward the tank without bothering to remove their filthy jungle fatigues and dusty boots, much to the dismay of the quartermaster sergeant who was running the shower point. I didn't interfere in the ensuing melee even though I knew I would catch hell for it from the battalion XO. We were all relieved to be out of the darkness of the primeval forest.

chapter seven

respite

Rest, rest perturbed spirit.
—WILLIAM SHAKESPEARE,
Hamlet

Charlie Company continued on standby as the brigade ready-reaction force for several days after the night airmobile operation. During this period, we were all undergoing the after-effects of the worst stress of our young lives. Men react differently to combat. Some troops became uncommunicative, their eyes fixed in a thousand-yard stare. Others were all bravado, telling their personal stories and trying to put the episodes of the battle together like pieces in a puzzle. Most carried captured AK-47s as trophies of war, and they were more than disappointed when our S-2 confiscated them; the grunts thought they would be permitted to ship the captured weapons home. More than a few of my men drank until they passed out in their bunkers. There was no shortage of hard liquor at FSB Concord, although it was banned, and beer was always available, courtesy of the battalion sergeant major. But liquor didn't stop the nightmares.

When the wounded who were not evacuated out of country returned to the company, everyone wanted to know the details of their hospital time. Were the nurses good-looking? Why couldn't they swing a period of recuperation in Japan? What was it like being dusted off? We were curious about the wounded, but we avoided the subject of death. None of us could conceive of his own death. That is, until the numbness began to wear off. Then we all began to experience fear once more.

A few days after the night airmobile assault, Lieutenant Colonel Mastoris notified me that I would have to give up one lieutenant to serve on the battalion staff as assistant S-4. I didn't know my lieutenants that well at this point, and it put me in a tough spot. Howard Tuber, 1st Platoon leader, was new and the only one of my platoon leaders that I had the opportunity to observe under fire. I recommended the Ohioan for the Bronze Star for valor. His leadership more than met the test. The 2d Platoon leader, soft-spoken Al Lenhardt, and his platoon were out on ambush on 31 January and never made contact. The 3d Platoon leader, Bob Stanley, was a sharp-looking lieutenant from Illinois. He was on R&R leave during Tet. Nevertheless, his platoon fought bravely, which indicated that he had trained them well. Paul Viola, who had several months of rifle-platoon experience, was the Mortar Platoon leader. Almost everyone took to this tall, amicable, twenty-four-year-old from Connecticut. The Mortar Platoon leader position was arguably the most important of all the platoon leader positions. The 81mm mortars gave the rifle company its own indirect-fire capability that could turn the tide of a battle. Viola and Jaynes ran Mortar Platoon like clockwork. Lieutenant Carl Frazier, a gung-ho Texan, was the Charlie Company XO and competently ran the administrative and logistic end of the company. They were all capable officers. It was a tough decision. I didn't want to show any favoritism, and none of the lieutenants volunteered to leave the company. I decided to have them draw straws. Al Lenhardt drew the short straw and took the staff position, which he executed admirably.

* * *

Heavy fighting continued in Cholon, Hue, and other areas of South Vietnam during the early part of February, and everyone thought we would be moved to one of those areas.

When the orders came, we were surprised to learn that our new AO was just a few kilometers east of the II Field Force perimeter at Long Binh.

On 8 February, the same day that Robert Kennedy first attacked the Johnson administration's policies on Vietnam, we moved by truck convoy to our new AO (area of operations), which was called South Uniontown. We were part of Operation Uniontown III. Charlie Company was relieved of its ready-reaction force mission, making it unlikely that we would be committed to action at a moment's notice. I breathed a sigh of relief at that news.

While our sister battalion, 3/7th Infantry, battled to secure the Phu Tho Racetrack in Cholon, Charlie Company spent five days situated within sight of the II Field Force perimeter wire. There was obvious concern about the possibility of another series of attacks in the Long Binh area.

Our area provided no cover or concealment, so we baked in the sun all day. The only shade available was from ponchos that we strung over our fighting positions. I kept thinking we should be trying to interdict the VC and NVA as they withdrew toward their sanctuaries in Cambodia. As time wore on, I became more skeptical about the second wave of attacks predicted for February. We had hurt them too badly during Tet.

On 18 February, we were given permission to move eastward to the edge of the jungle. Charlie Company established a position along a stream. We built a two-rope bridge across the stream and constructed our bunkers on the edge of a large clearing in the jungle. We had good fields of fire across the clearing and plenty of timber to construct overhead cover for our bunkers. I requisitioned a supply of sandbags and concertina wire to complete the work.

Our position was pleasant. The men swam and fished in the stream. We soon realized that the best piece of fishing tackle was the hand grenade. Seconds after someone tossed a grenade in the water, dozens of fish floated belly-up on the surface. Within minutes there were enough fish for a first-class fish fry.

It was as if we were trying to recapture the lost innocence of our boyhood years. During the day it was like a summer camping trip, but as darkness descended, all eyes focused on the green galleries of bamboo at the edge of the clearing beyond our perimeter.

I ordered listening posts (LPs) in front of each platoon's position. Two men from each platoon crept forward into the bamboo thickets, laying commo wire for their sound-powered telephones. Wire provided a reliable means of communicating with our LPs, whose mission was to provide early warning of any enemy approach. LP was not a popular assignment among the grunts. It was difficult to see anything in the darkness, but sound carries a long way at night, and in the damp stillness of the jungle you can hear the slightest movement, including creatures slithering and rustling through the vegetation. No breezes penetrated the tangled foliage, and mosquitoes attack with a vengeance. Minutes pass like hours in the damp, sodden jungle. If an enemy attack was detected, the LPs were supposed to withdraw to the perimeter after giving the warning, a risky maneuver at best.

The days were more pleasant. We sent out squad-size daylight patrols, but there was no sign of the enemy. We test-fired our weapons, including two 60mm mortars that Viola procured. These mortars dated back to World War II and were much lighter than the company's 81s, which were too heavy to carry on jungle operations and had to be flown in to company night defensive positions, provided that an

LZ was nearby. The Mortar Platoon soldiers were more than pleased with the lightweight 60mm mortars and had no problem becoming proficient with them.

One afternoon two troopers from an engineer outfit appeared on a ridgeline overlooking our position while Mortar Platoon was practicing with the new mortars. The engineers spotted some of our men and mistook them for VC. They opened fire with their M16s. More than a little annoyed, I ordered Mortar Platoon to fire a 60mm mortar round close to, but a safe distance from, the engineers' location. We saw the round strike about a hundred meters short of the ridgeline. The engineers were last seen scrambling into their jeep and leaving the ridgeline in a cloud of dust.

The morale of the company continued to improve during this period, and there was more bonding within the CP group itself. A combat commander must rely heavily on communications to command and control his unit. Communications determines whether or not a unit receives fire support, medevac support, and resupply. Therefore, a commander's RTOs are very important and critical people for him. Being an RTO was a tough job in Vietnam, and a dangerous one. There were higher casualty rates among RTOs, because they were easily identified by the radios and antennas that they carried. Their work was also demanding, both mentally and physically. An RTO, usually a specialist fourth class, would often find himself talking directly to a battalion or brigade commander while his company commander maneuvered his platoons. Therefore, these soldiers had to be articulate, intelligent, and knowledgeable about the tactical situation at all times.

When I assumed command of Charlie Company, I inherited an RTO, a kid from Florida, who lacked the maturity for the job. I replaced him with Bob Archibald, the company jeep driver, before Tet. This easygoing twenty-three-year-old Californian proved himself beyond any doubt during the Tet fighting, and was well liked by just about everyone in the company.

Cliff Kaylor was the senior RTO. He had been well trained by my commo chief, Larry Abel, who had previously held the job. Kaylor held one of the most responsible jobs in the company. During the heaviest periods of fighting at Ho Nai village, he had demonstrated a solid grasp of the tactical situation and was able to describe it for the battalion commander while I directed the fight. I respected his competence, but we were at war from the start. Cliff Kaylor had attended Purdue and Ohio State before joining the Army. He had a cynical view of the war and wasn't shy about expressing it. This irritated me, but I couldn't spare him. As my time in Vietnam passed, I would be at war with myself over some of these same issues.

First Sergeant George Holmes, more than anyone, kept things running on an even keel. His responsibilities extended from the troops in the field to those in the rear. Some first sergeants spent most of their time at the base camp. Holmes and I knew that wouldn't work for Charlie Company. From my perspective, the company XO, assisted by our rear-detachment NCO, Sergeant Verania, could run the show in the rear. I wanted Holmes at my side while we were on operation because he was the most experienced combat veteran in the company, having survived Korea and a previous tour in Vietnam. He was also someone I could talk to. I didn't want to become too familiar with the other members of the command group; a certain level of aloofness is seen as a positive trait in military leadership.

As there was little activity in our area, I sent several soldiers to Vung Tau on in-country R&R. Holmes also rotated the NCOs, a few at a time, back to main base camp for overnight breaks. Most spent the evening drinking at the NCO club and stayed out of serious trouble. There was, however, one exception. PSG Cliff Jaynes went to one of the Long Binh–based aviation outfits to look up an old NCO buddy. Both men had been dropped from warrant officer flight school a week prior to graduation and were shipped out to Vietnam. After a few beers, Jaynes and his buddy decided to take a night joy ride in one of the Hueys. They flew around for about an hour and returned the helicopter safely to base. The whole episode was kept in NCO channels. Holmes and the Warrior battalion sergeant major had to go see the aviation battalion sergeant major to convince him that Jaynes's career was worth saving. Jaynes was in for the Silver Star and had a solid reputation. Holmes didn't tell me about it until months later. The NCOs got it right. Jaynes was too good a man to lose.

February wore on. An engineer outfit was clearing jungle near our location with Rome Plows. These huge bulldozers with angular tree-cutting blades took sniper fire on an almost daily basis, and they finally asked for our help. I sent patrols into their area to eliminate the snipers, but without any success. Frustrated, I requested a combat tracker team. The expert tracker and his dog accompanied one patrol. On 21 February, Charlie Company was ordered back to the 199th base camp. Our respite was over.

chapter eight

stand-down

Even victors are by victories undone.
—JOHN DRYDEN,
"To My Honored Kinsman"

We were told to expect a three-day stand-down at Camp Frenzell-Jones. Tet hadn't slowed the construction of new facilities; there was a new officers club, new quarters for the brigade commander, a new PX, and a club for the enlisted men. When I had arrived in-country, the officers club was housed in a large Army tent with makeshift furniture. Now the club was in a wooden building with a regular bar, complete with bar stools, a mirror, a small stage, and a stereo system. Adjacent to the new club was the brigade commander's air-conditioned bungalow. The dusty roads and sandbagged bunkers along the perimeter were the only reminders that the camp was in a war zone.

I had a few beers that evening with some other officers from the battalion. Most of us had cleaned ourselves up a bit, but we stood out in sharp contrast to the staff officers in their starched and ironed jungle fatigues and spit-shined jungle boots. The staffers slowly moved from the bar to tables in the rear of the room as we took over the bar stools. It was apparent that they resented us taking over their turf, but they accepted our temporary incursion with resignation. After all, they knew it was only for a night or two.

I returned to my bunk in the company's barracks around midnight. The platoon leaders and I shared a room on the second floor. About an hour later, the VC mortared the base camp. All of the incoming rounds landed in the Warrior battalion area. We were the only infantry battalion on stand-down in the base camp, and the VC knew it. The enemy rarely targeted the rear-detachment barracks. Similarly, facilities such as the PX and clubs that provided employment for Vietnamese day workers were not priority targets.

When the attack began I grabbed my CAR15 and dashed out onto the second-floor landing. Still half asleep, I missed the stairway and fell about fifteen feet to the ground. I landed with a jarring thud and lay spread-eagled on the ground with the wind knocked out of me. As I gasped for air, two of my men dragged me into the bunker. I was more than a little embarrassed at my own clumsiness. Charlie Company didn't suffer any casualties, but there were some wounded in the battalion.

The next morning I had breakfast with the 7th Support Battalion commander, Lt. Col. Al Abelson. We had met at the club the night before, where he had extended an invitation for breakfast. Abelson was responsible for the perimeter defense of the base camp and was more than grateful that Charlie Company had preempted the enemy's attack on the base during Tet. He knew that the base camp's defenders, mainly mechanics, supply clerks, and cooks, wouldn't have stood a chance against the enemy's battle-hardened troops.

Abelson lived in a bungalow just like the general's. The house had a fully equipped kitchen, and Abelson had his own cook. Not bad for a lieutenant colonel, I thought. The bungalow was air-conditioned and completely furnished with American civilian furniture. Abelson's previous job was at the Saigon port, where he was in charge of all supplies and equipment arriving by sea. He knew the in-country logistic system and how to procure anything the brigade needed. Abelson told me to ask the cook for anything I wanted for breakfast. I had steak and eggs. Walking back to my orderly room, I began to reflect on the different dimensions of this war.

Later that morning, Brig. Gen. Bob Forbes came down to our battalion area for an awards ceremony. He pinned Purple Hearts to the soldiers who had been wounded during Tet, and also awarded several Bronze Stars and Army Commendation Medals for valor. Higher awards such as the Silver Star and Distinguished Service Cross were pending approval at higher headquarters.

After the ceremony, the battalion adjutant told me I was getting a new lieutenant to fill a platoon leader vacancy in 2d Platoon. Lieutenant Mike Hinkley, a quiet twenty-two-year-old New Hampshire native, reported an hour later. Mike had graduated from college and had considered joining the Navy before an Army recruiter signed him up for OCS. After briefing him, I introduced him to his platoon sergeant, thirty-six-year-old SSgt. Thomas Lawrence.

That same afternoon our stand-down was cut short, and the battalion was ordered to leave the base camp. Most of the men were hungover and angry that the stand-down lasted only one night. I shared their disappointment, but I couldn't show it.

As we prepared to move out, I received a call at the orderly room that Colonel Davison, our deputy brigade commander, wanted to see Paul Viola, my Mortar Platoon leader, and three men from his platoon. Lieutenant Viola was nervous and concerned about any blemish on his record. He was married, and he was thinking about becoming a career Army officer. As it turned out, Viola had put in a priority-one requisition for enough jungle boots to reshoe his entire platoon. Priority-one requisitions normally were reserved for combat-essential items such as weapons and ammo. Davison wanted have a look at some of Viola's men's boots before he signed off on the supply requisition. The troops got their new jungle boots.

* * *

Charlie Company marched down the main road toward the main gate of the base camp. The troops looked gaunt and weary. Their freshly laundered jungle fatigues hung loosely on their rawboned frames. Dust rolled off our boot tops as we marched. It wasn't hard to distinguish the Charlie Company grunts from the rear-echelon troops we passed along the way. None of us wore pressed fatigues or spit-shined boots like theirs, and all of us except the most recent replacements had sunburned arms and faces disfigured by infected bamboo scratches and insect bites. The troops jeered and traded insults with the base-camp soldiers we passed. We marched on.

Our route of march took us through the village of Ho Nai, where we fought during Tet, and then east along Highway 1. We then marched north on a trail that led into our new AO. We had been over this same terrain in January; it was familiar. We passed a corpse sprawled in a ditch alongside a dirt road. The dead man, a Vietnamese, had a noose around his neck. South Vietnamese civilians in the area told us that the man was a VC political cadre member who had been lynched by an angry mob of villagers after the VC main force units withdrew from the area. During Tet, twelve prominent villagers had been dragged out of their beds and shot by VC. Few, if any, of us really understood the war from the Vietnamese perspective.

After a few days it became apparent that we weren't accomplishing much in this area besides providing security for the Long Binh base area. The badly mauled VC main force units had withdrawn into their sanctuaries in war zones C and D. I didn't understand why we were not pursuing them.

Charlie Company had a close call one night while occupying a position close to where we had surprised the enemy battalion during the night of 31 January. I was walking around checking the perimeter just after dark when we suddenly came under heavy small-arms fire. I dove to the ground and immediately looked around for better cover. Rounds were passing no more than a few inches over my body. The fire was coming from a road that led into the village. The Charlie Company grunts returned the fire coming from the road and quickly gained fire superiority. Then I began to hear some shouting in broken English.

"Cease fire, GI. Cease fire!"

I realized that we had been taking friendly fire. Fortunately, no one was hit.

A Vietnamese PF patrol moving down the road had mistaken us for VC. No one had briefed the patrol that our NDP was near the village. This was hard for me to swallow because our brigade I&R Platoon was located in the same compound as the PF unit, and one of their sergeants was with the patrol.

The I&R Platoon leader came to our location the next morning. I chewed the lieutenant out for not briefing the PF patrol about our location, and told him that I would mortar the hell out of the PF platoon compound if another incident like this occurred. Since his own outfit was located at the PF headquarters, he took my threat seriously and reported it to brigade headquarters. I was reprimanded, but the point was already made. It didn't happen again.

The friendly fire incident notwithstanding, I had other reasons for wanting to leave this area. For starters, it was unhealthy. The stench of death was still on the land even though the bodies of enemy soldiers killed during Tet had been bulldozed into mass graves three weeks earlier. Furthermore, the village was a major distraction for the troops. The villagers were trying to scrounge anything they could from us to repair their houses. Also, it didn't take long for the prostitutes to get back to business. Every morning a couple of short-time girls accompanied by a betel-nut-chewing mamasan set up business in the bushes near our patrol base. I didn't get much cooperation from the NCOs in running the whores off. First Sergeant Holmes told me not to worry about it. He kept a large supply of condoms in his rucksack and dispensed them liberally to the troops. We reached a compromise. The prostitutes had to be out of the area before evening chow.

The only advantage of being near the base camp was that we received hot chow once a day. The battalion mess section trucked out Mermite cans of hot rations to our field location. We also received cold sodas, two cans of beer per man, and a daily sundry pack containing cigarettes, candy, soap, and toothpaste. That was great for morale, but I felt that the company was starting to lose its combat edge. A number of seasoned veterans had rotated back to the States since Tet, and their replacements had yet to make an airmobile assault on an LZ and then hump five or more kilometers through dense jungle to reach an objective. More important, the new men had never been under enemy fire.

All this was about to change.

chapter nine

valley forge

Ship me somewheres east of Suez, where the best is like
the worst, / Where there aren't no Ten Commandments
an' a man can raise a thirst.

—RUDYARD KIPLING,
"Mandalay"

On 9 March 1968, the 199th Light Infantry Brigade in-
augurated Operation Valley Forge. We were finally going
on the offensive. The operation plan called for the Warrior
battalion, 4/12th Infantry, to insert three rifle companies
into landing zones south of Highway 1, about twenty-five
miles east of Bien Hoa. After landing, the light infantry
companies were to sweep east through the jungle to link up
with units from the 2d Squadron, 11th Armored Cavalry
Regiment. The operation planners were hopeful that an enemy battalion known to be operating in the area would be
trapped between the converging light infantry and cavalry
units.

Charlie Company's LZ was softened up with artillery
and gunship fire, and we went in with door gunners blazing away with their M60s. I looked at my new FO, Lt. Paul
Lange, who sat cross-legged next to the door of the chopper. His face was deathly pale. This was his first combat
assault, and he was completely unnerved by the experience.

The bamboo along the edges of the LZ was smoldering
by the time we landed. When running through the smoke
and dust kicked up by the rotor blades, it was difficult to
tell if the *crack*s and *pop*s we heard were incoming fire or

the burning bamboo. Fortunately, the assault was unopposed.

By monitoring the battalion radio net I learned that the other insertions all went as planned. None of the LZs was hot.

Delta Company's LZ was closest to ours, and Charlie and Delta companies were supposed to move on parallel axes toward the armored cavalry units. Captain Jim Dabney was the new commander of Delta Company. He had spent a day and night with Charlie Company before assuming command. I liked him from the start. Jim had been wounded while leading a company in the 9th Infantry Division. General Forbes knew Dabney from the 9th Division and had him reassigned to the 199th when his wounds healed.

Neither Jim nor I had high expectations that the enemy battalion, if it was still in this area, was going to be caught napping while the infantry and cavalry units closed in. If the enemy wanted to fight, they would occupy well-prepared ambush positions and wait for us to stumble into them. If the enemy commander wasn't looking for a fight, he would have his unit break down into elements of five or six men and melt away into the jungle. On a sweep like this, an infantry company's frontage while moving through dense jungle was only about a hundred yards. By moving quickly and quietly, small groups of VC had no difficulty evading us in the jungle. We had to move much slower to maintain security and avoid being ambushed.

Typically, we would move a couple hundred yards, stop, and send out small cloverleaf patrols to our front and flanks to ensure that we weren't walking into an ambush. These three-man patrols moved out ahead and to the flanks of each platoon to a distance of about seventy-five to one hundred meters, and then swung around in a cloverleaf pattern, returning to their platoon at the end of the sweep.

Moving on trails was quicker than moving cross-country,

but we almost never followed trails. The enemy set up ambushes and command-detonated mines and booby traps on trail networks. Consequently, we moved on jungle tracks and trails only under extreme circumstances.

Senior officers in the chain of command poorly understood these tactics. They just didn't get it. Flying hundreds of feet above us, the colonels and generals became impatient when it took us hours to traverse a couple of kilometers. The jungle is much less intimidating when you're five hundred feet above it, and very few senior officers ever crawled on hands and knees through a bamboo thicket or cut their way through secondary jungle growth with a machete.

Lieutenant Colonel Mastoris wanted Charlie and Delta companies to link up with the 11th Armored Cavalry units before nightfall. The linkup point was eight kilometers to our east. By midafternoon I knew we'd never make our objective by nightfall. By early evening we had reached a clearing large enough to use as an LZ. We were running out of water, and I wanted to fly in my 81mm mortars for the night. Mastoris agreed and directed Jim Dabney to move his company into the same LZ.

Two companies sharing the same night defensive position apparently raised some command-and-control issues for Mastoris. Dabney was slightly senior to me by date of rank, but I really don't think Mastoris knew him well enough to put him in charge at this point. Instead, Mastoris decided to fly in Maj. Ed Kelley, the battalion XO, with a couple of RTOs to form a battalion field CP at the LZ. I thought it was unnecessary. Kelley was a good XO in the rear, but to my knowledge had never spent a night in the bush. Dabney and I had already coordinated our defensive positions when he arrived.

We had dug in along a two-company perimeter around the LZ with interlocking fires. Both companies sent out night ambush patrols and listening posts. We weren't going to be taken by surprise that night. After Jim and I briefed Kelley on our defensive measures, he had his small command group set up about fifty yards from my CP foxhole. I noticed that the battalion CP group was not digging in.

As my RTOs unpacked their rucksacks, I saw Kaylor removing two fifths of Johnny Walker Red from his pack. He quickly covered them with his poncho liner when he saw me looking in his direction.

"Kaylor, what in the hell do you think you're doing with that whiskey out here in the bush?"

Kaylor responded sheepishly. "Well, Sir, I bought two fifths to drink during our stand-down that they screwed us out of. There was no place to store it in the rear, and I couldn't see wasting good liquor."

"Bring those two bottles over here and pour them out on the ground," I said sternly, trying not to crack a smile.

"You know I wasn't going to drink this stuff in the field," he said as he upended the bottles.

I could hear the guffaws coming from Bob Archibald, Holmes, and the FO as Kaylor poured.

Around midnight the cavalry troop that we were supposed to have linked up with that day came under attack by a company-size VC force. We were close enough to hear the gunfire, and monitored the fight on our battalion radio net. The VC crept close enough to the cavalry perimeter to knock out an M48A3 tank with their first RPG round, killing or wounding the entire crew. They also badly damaged an ACAV. It was touch-and-go for a while, but the cavalry outfit soon gained fire superiority with their .50-caliber machine guns and 90mm tank guns. The enemy ground attack faltered when it reached the triple rolls of concertina wire around the cavalry perimeter. The machine-gun fire and Claymores ripped them apart. When the helicopter gunships arrived on the scene, the enemy withdrew to the jungle.

Right in the middle of the cavalry fight, Major Kelley and his RTOs came stumbling through the brush into my CP area. It was apparent that Kelley had second thoughts about not digging in. He told me that I was in charge of the ground defense of the perimeter if we got hit, and that he would keep in communications with our battalion commander. He also said it would probably be better if he stayed in my CP area. Somewhat amused, I pointed out an area and suggested he direct his RTOs to start digging in. They weren't carrying entrenching tools, so Holmes and I lent them ours. Fortunately, our position wasn't attacked that night. This is the first and last time I recall a field-grade officer in our battalion spending the night with a rifle company on a field operation.

The night attack on the 2/11th Cavalry troop pretty much confirmed that an enemy base camp was somewhere in our new AO. The Warrior battalion, along with the cavalry, began to search for it. An air cavalry outfit joined the hunt. After four and a half days of sweeping the jungle, the air cavalry's scouts in their OH-6 light observation helicopters located the enemy base camp. Cobra gunships rolled in with rocket and minigun runs on the heavily fortified bunkers, and a tactical air strike was requested.

Charlie Company was the closest ground unit to the base camp, about two kilometers away, and we could hear the strikes going in. Mastoris radioed the coordinates and indicated that we were to go to the scene of the action as soon as possible. No LZs were in the area, so we had to hump it. We began the march with less than a canteen of water per man. It took us more than an hour to make the first kilometer, and we were pushing hard. An airstrike was in progress. We could hear the high-performance aircraft busting bunkers with five-hundred-pound bombs and napalm.

I had no idea of the layout of the bunker complex, so I didn't know what to expect as we drew closer. Another hour of movement brought us to the base of a hill. We still had no contact, but artillery was now firing into the bunker complex. Big stuff, 155mm and 8-inch howitzers.

I called up my platoon leaders and laid out a plan. Mike Hinkley's 2d Platoon was to assault on the left and Bob Stanley's 3d Platoon was to take the right. Hinkley was my greenest platoon leader; he needed to get his feet wet. Lieutenant Tuber's 1st Platoon would be in reserve.

We moved out slowly and I directed Paul Lange, my new FO, to shift the artillery fire to the reverse slope of the hill.

As we moved forward up the hill, we could see the enemy bunkers. The foliage wasn't too thick. I was surprised that we still weren't taking any fire. There were communications and fighting trenches running from bunker to bunker. The VC usually fought from these trenches with grenades, RPGs, and Claymores, just as they did from the bunkers, but the entire bunker complex was torn up badly by the air strikes. The smell of smoke, cordite, and napalm hung in the air. Unignited globs of napalm hung on some of the tree limbs.

Charlie Company's lead elements now crawled into the fighting trenches and lobbed hand grenades into the bunker apertures. There was no enemy resistance. It soon became evident that the enemy, or what was left of them, had cleared out before our arrival. We found several bodies and pieces of bodies along with some ammunition and documents, but that was it. I breathed a sigh of relief. Apparently, the VC company had been pretty badly mauled in the night attack on the cavalry, and the remnants had returned to this base camp. We found a lot of bloody bandages and other medical supplies. Evidently, the VC didn't have the strength to put up a good fight, so they pulled out after the air strikes. I breathed another sigh of relief.

While I was examining some of the bunkers, a new soldier from 1st Platoon approached me; he was holding an object in his hands.

"Hey, Captain, take a look at this thing I found!" When the man got within about six paces of me, I recognized the object. It was a gray metal spherical object about the size of a baseball—an unexploded cluster bomblet.

"Stop where you are!" He stopped. "Now set that thing gently on the ground, and start backing off real slow," I instructed him as I backed off. Fortunately, the bomb didn't explode, and we later detonated it with C4 plastic explosives.

It was getting late in the day, so I looked at my map for an NDP. There were no LZs nearby, and we badly needed a resupply of water. We moved a few hundred meters down a ridgeline and began to cut an LZ. The trees were huge, thirty to forty feet high, and hardwood. Each platoon carried a chainsaw, but the blades were dull. While the LZ detail worked away with their chainsaws, the rest of the men began digging in. Suddenly, one of the huge trees crashed to the ground. It fell in the wrong direction and landed on several men from 3d Platoon who were digging a fighting position. Platoon Sergeant Wyers was one of the unlucky men; he suffered two fractured vertebrae. At age thirty-four, Wyers's stint with Charlie Company was over. Two other men also were injured.

We called for a medevac and continued cutting. We finally felled enough trees for a single-ship LZ, but the helicopter would have to hover over the clearing and drop almost straight down.

When a resupply ship arrived before the medevac, I tried to guide the pilot into the LZ. He circled the area several times, then said he wouldn't risk it. By this time our water situation was really critical. The pilot said he would have to drop the water and rations to us. His crew chief began throwing five-gallon plastic jugs of water and cases of C rations out of the hovering Huey. All the plastic water containers splattered when they hit the ground.

A medevac helicopter arrived a few minutes later, and it dropped right down into the small LZ. After the injured men were loaded, he took off again without incident. The dust-off units had some of the best pilots in Vietnam.

Before dark a tank platoon from the 2/11th Armored Cavalry rolled into our NDP. While directing the tanks into positions around the perimeter, I noted that each one carried several five-gallon cans of water. I asked the platoon leader if he could spare us any water. He said he could only spare us two cans, ten gallons. This amount didn't stretch far for the 120 men I had in the company, so I ordered each platoon to send out a patrol to look for a stream. They all reported the same thing: There wasn't any water nearby. The company spent an uneasy night. We were too exhausted and dehydrated to sleep well.

At dawn the grunts rolled out of their poncho liners, their jungle fatigues still damp from the previous day's perspiration. As I drained the last bit of juice from a C ration can of sliced peaches, the driver of the M48A3 tank closest to the CP cranked its 690-horsepower engine. I was standing about fifteen meters behind the tank, as the hot exhaust fumes blew toward me. The other four tanks around the perimeter were cranking up as well. Suddenly, the five-ton tank near us lurched into reverse. The CP group was right in its path. Grabbing their radios and M16s, Kaylor and Archibald scrambled to get out of the way as the tank crashed through the undergrowth. Kaylor's steel helmet, which he had left on the ground, was crushed by the tank's tread.

I shouted at the tank commander to stop, but the engine noise drowned out all the shouting. Waving my arms wildly, I finally attracted the attention of the tank platoon leader, who was sitting in the tank's cupola. The tank jerked to a stop a few feet from the CP.

Enraged, I climbed up onto the deck of the tank. Working my way around the hot engine grates I moved toward the commander's cupola. The lieutenant removed his tanker's helmet as I shouted over the roar of the engine, "What in the hell do you think you're doing, Lieutenant?"

The wide-eyed lieutenant must have seen the blood in my eyes. He stammered. "We got orders from our commander to move out, Sir. Sorry, we didn't know you were set up right behind us."

"Listen. You nearly ran over my CP group. Didn't you ever hear of using a ground guide when you're in a bivouac area?"

Still infuriated, but trying to get control of my emotions, I ordered the armor lieutenant to radio his other tank commanders and tell them to use ground guides until they were clear of our perimeter. I wasn't sorry to see the tankers depart. The day wasn't off to a good start.

The morning haze was lifting as we hefted our rucksacks and moved out toward our day's objective, an LZ about five kilometers away. All morning we broke our way through the secondary growth jungle, trudging through dry streambeds and laboring awkwardly up the slopes of the hills. Thorny bushes and wait-a-minute vines impeded each man's progress by catching on their rifles and clothing. Some men muttered curses as they thrashed their way through the brush, while others saved their breath and stumbled on in silence. Everyone, including the men in my CP group, was exhausted by midmorning. I noticed that my RTOs were breathing heavily under the weight of their rucksacks and radios, and their faces were turning red from the sun and exertion. The usual playful bantering between Kaylor and Archibald was absent as they trudged on sullenly, one behind the other. No one was talking. The sunlight and heat were too oppressive.

Charlie Company's four platoons were strung out in two columns, each about a hundred meters long. Concerned about heat casualties, I rested the men fifteen minutes every hour. Everyone was dehydrated. Most of the men were carrying at least fifty pounds of equipment distributed between their rucksacks and web gear. Attached to their web gear were two canteens; two ammo pouches, each containing several magazines of 5.56mm ammo; and two or three grenades. Rucksacks were crammed with C rations, extra ammo, poncho liners, and Claymore mines, and each soldier also carried extra belted 7.62mm ammo for the M60 machine guns.

Despite the exertion required to keep moving, I noticed that the men all were carrying their rifles at the ready. During brief halts, most of the men stood in a partial crouch, their backs aching while they waited for the column to move forward. Some appeared close to collapse. Concerned about dehydration and heat exhaustion, I halted the column for a long break. Wearily, the men flopped down to rest motionless for several moments. First Sergeant Holmes shared the last of his water with me.

When I noticed that the exhausted men were falling asleep, I ordered the company to move out. The men in the CP group began to grumble, which was a bad example for the rest of the company.

"Come on!" I chided them. "On your feet, and quit your bitching. You're setting a lousy example for the others. We got a long way to go."

The troops nearby stared at me resentfully. They had to

have someone to blame for their thirst and fatigue, and I was the one.

We plodded on much more slowly now. A few men were nearing collapse, so we had to pool our remaining water to cool them down. Their squad leaders unloaded the men's rucksacks and divided up their ammunition and rations among the other squad members. I spotted a 90mm recoilless rifle gunner who was stumbling under his twenty-five-pound weapon. I grabbed the weapon from the man and lifted it to my shoulders to carry it for a while.

By 1500 hours, we had a couple of heat casualties in each platoon. The men improvised stretchers by cutting small saplings for the poles and stretching their ponchos over them. I slowed the pace yet again and ordered a halt about every fifteen minutes. Finally, we hit a trail that ran in the direction of the LZ. Normally, we avoided moving on trails, but we needed to get to a water supply fast. The lead platoon sent out a point squad with a couple of M60 machine guns.

Alert to the possibility of an ambush, we moved cautiously down the trail toward the LZ. Our luck held, and the point squad broke into the large clearing about 1600 hours. The rest of the exhausted men followed. The battalion reconnaissance platoon had secured the LZ, and a couple of sorties of resupply helicopters had already landed with water and C rations.

I had First Sergeant Holmes set up a water point after we claimed our share of the plastic water jugs. The rear platoons were still strung out along the trail and hadn't yet closed, so I wouldn't allow any of the water to be distributed. I didn't want to start a stampede. I spotted Cliff Kaylor hovering over one of the water jugs.

"Kaylor, I'll have to shoot you if you try to drink any of that water," I admonished him jokingly. He didn't think I was joking and murmured something at me under his breath.

The rear platoon finally staggered into the bright sunlight of the LZ. Some of the men were limping on sore feet, and everyone was chafed and sunburned. After the platoon leaders moved their men into their assigned defensive sectors, I opened the water point. The men were permitted to fill two canteens each, one squad at a time at the water point. First Sergeant Holmes made sure not a drop of the precious liquid was spilled in the process. Some of the men in line at the water point mumbled about the delay, but every man received his fair share. As the water was being distributed, a medevac ship arrived to evacuate the heat casualties. Then we dug in and night descended. It had been a hell of a long march.

Operation Valley Forge ended on 17 March, one day after Sen. Robert Kennedy announced his candidacy for the Democratic presidential nomination. We hoped for a stand-down at the brigade main base camp, but instead the Warrior battalion immediately embarked on a series of airmobile assaults into southern War Zone D. The Warrior battalion headquarters and Charlie Battery, 2/40th Artillery, moved into FSB Lois, where they relieved the 2/506th Infantry, 101st Airborne. There was also a mixed battery of 155mm and 8-inch self-propelled howitzers at the small fire base.

Charlie Company was to secure FSB Lois during this new operation, designated Operation Box Springs. We airmobiled into the fire base on 21 March.

FSB Lois was too small for the number of artillery pieces positioned on it. Moreover, it was poorly constructed. We had to rebuild most of the existing perimeter bunkers and add overhead cover. I was also concerned about how the jungle grew almost to the perimeter wire. What had the engineers been doing with their bulldozer, I wondered?

We built the company CP bunker right beside a 105mm howitzer position. There wasn't much space left. Just before dusk I decided to take my first shower in a couple of weeks. Sonny McGlinchy, the company field supply sergeant, had scrounged an Australian canvas shower bag from somewhere and hung it up in a tree near the CP. I was just soaping up under the shower when an artillery marking round burst in the air about one hundred feet above the fire base. I took off stark naked for the CP bunker, about ten meters away, fully aware of what was coming next. Seconds later, five high-explosive 105mm howitzer rounds slammed into the base. Luckily, most of the troops were in their bunkers. Only two men were wounded by the friendly fire. It could have been much worse.

We soon learned that the artillery was fired by the 101st Airborne Division. The 101st Artillery sometimes fired missions into abandoned fire bases, because the VC often moved in and scrounged any materials left behind. In this case, the 101st Division Artillery (DIVARTY) claimed that no one had told them that our battalion occupied the base. Outraged at the screwup, our brigade deputy commander, Colonel Davison, paid a visit to 101st Headquarters and demanded an investigation of the incident.

The following day, Delta Company found a VC tunnel complex and uncovered a cache of 122mm rockets and their launchers, along with a number of other weapons. The captured weapons were moved to the fire base, and a group of VIPs and reporters flew in to look at the prizes.

Toward evening a Huey with some brass and reporters on board was lifting off the base helipad when the pilot clipped a tree with his main rotor blade. The helicopter plunged about ten feet to the ground and started to burn. Fortunately, the crew and passengers escaped uninjured. We weren't able to extinguish the flames, and the helicopter was a total loss. Everyone took cover in their bunkers when the M60 machine-gun ammunition began cooking off. It was quite a fireworks display!

We stayed on the fire base another four days. There were no signs of any major enemy units in the area, so on 26 March we were ordered to close the fire base. The battalion headquarters and Charlie Battery, 2/40th, moved by air back to the main base at Long Binh, but Charlie Company was ordered to move overland to provide security for a convoy of self-propelled 155mm and 8-inch howitzers. A squad from the 87th Engineer Company and a platoon from D Troop, 17th Cavalry, were attached to provide additional security for the convoy.

Our planned route followed a dirt road that led southwest from FSB Lois toward the town of Tan Uyen. From Tan Uyen, the convoy would follow Highway 314 south along the Dong Nai River to Bien Hoa. From Bien Hoa, it was just a few miles into our base at Long Binh.

The first part of the march was by far the most dangerous. We knew the dirt road was mined. An ACAV and a self-propelled howitzer had been destroyed on the move into the fire base. To clear the road, I ordered 1st Platoon and the engineer squad to sweep ahead of the convoy using mine detectors. The other Charlie Company platoons would move on foot along the flanks of the road to prevent an ambush.

As the convoy prepared to depart, the engineer platoon leader told me that his bulldozer wouldn't start. I radioed the battalion TOC for instructions. I knew that the bulldozer could be airlifted by a CH-54 helicopter if the tracks were removed. No CH-54s were available. I was told to have the engineers destroy their dozer in place. It would be stripped for parts by the VC if we left it behind.

The engineers packed the engine compartment with C-plastic explosives and lit a time fuse just as the convoy cleared FSB Lois. I noticed Dale Tracy from my CP group just shaking his head in disgust when we heard the explosion.

"What's wrong with you?" I asked.

"My dad is in the lumber business back in Washington

state, and it would take him a lifetime to buy one of those. What a waste," he observed.

The convoy inched forward along as the mine-detector teams swept the road fifty yards ahead of the lead vehicle. The mine-detector teams located two Soviet antitank mines buried under the dirt within five hundred meters of the fire support base. We halted the convoy and the engineers blew the mines in place.

We moved out again, but our progress was painstakingly slow. Finally, we reached an area where the Rome Plows had cleared the brush back about seventy-five meters on both sides of the road. I thought that we'd never even make it to Tan Uyen by dark if we didn't get moving. Moving at night through War Zone D with a convoy of vehicles like this one was an open invitation to disaster. I told the lead ACAV commander to pull his vehicles off to the cleared area next to the road and move parallel to it. The rest of the convoy followed, with Charlie Company mounted on the tracked vehicles. Fortunately, the enemy had mined only the road and not the shoulders.

We reached Tan Uyen and the paved Highway 314 before dark. Then the convoy really picked up speed and rolled south toward Bien Hoa. By 2000 hours, we were back at the main brigade base camp.

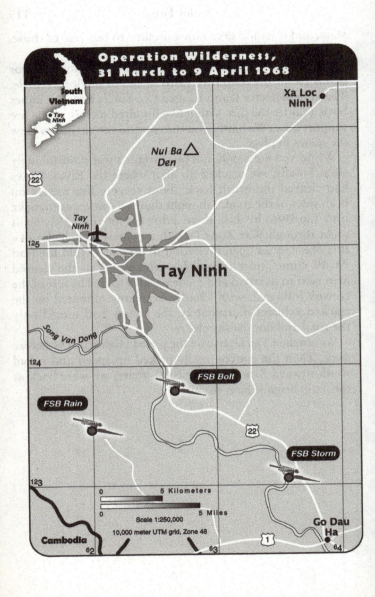

**Operation Wilderness,
31 March to 9 April 1968**

South Vietnam

Tay Ninh

Xa Loc Ninh

Nui Ba Den

22

Tay Ninh

Tay Ninh

Song Van Dong

FSB Bolt

FSB Rain

22

FSB Storm

125

124

123

62   63   64

Cambodia

Go Dau Ha

1

0   5 Kilometers
0   5 Miles
Scale 1:250,000
10,000 meter UTM grid, Zone 48

chapter ten

wilderness

With a host of furious fancies,
Whereof I am commander;
With a burning spear,
And a horse of air,
To the wilderness I wander.
—"Tom O'Bedlam's Song"

Operation Wilderness

After leaving FSB Lois, we had a two-day stand-down at the brigade's main base camp in Long Binh. The grunts and rear-echelon troops fought at the enlisted club. The officers club wasn't much calmer. An FO with the Warrior battalion started a fight with a group of officers over a seat at the bar. He had completed his time as FO with Bravo Company and was to assume new duties as a battery XO. He was charged with being drunk and disorderly, and received nonjudicial punishment under Article 15 of the UCMJ. Realizing his chances for a career were over, he asked to stay with the Warrior battalion as an FO until his tour was over. He was a superb FO.

On 30 March, Lieutenant Colonel Mastoris briefed us on our next operation. We had heard rumors that the brigade was about to move north to the Song Be area. This would be the first time the brigade moved that far north. Song Be was in Charlie country. We all knew that.

We were surprised when Mastoris told us that we were moving to the Tay Ninh area, not to Song Be as we thought. Our new AO was west of Tay Ninh, just a few kilometers from the Cambodian border. The 199th would be under the operational control of the 25th Infantry Division out of Cu Chi. According to our S-2, large NVA and VC base areas—and possibly COSVN, the enemy high-command headquarters—were just across the Cambodian border. NVA tanks had been reported in Cambodia, too. Mastoris instructed us to carry plenty of M72 LAWs in addition to our 90mm recoilless rifles, which we often left behind due to the weight of the weapon and its ammunition. This time, however, we prepared for the worst.

The Warrior battalion commenced movement on 31 March, the same day that Lyndon Johnson announced that he was unilaterally halting the bombing of North Vietnam and would not seek reelection in the fall. I was stunned when I heard the announcement. Here we were about to undertake a major operation on the Cambodian border— our biggest so far—and our commander-in-chief was calling it quits. We had heard about the riots and protests back in the World, but we were shocked that LBJ was not going to see this war through. It was demoralizing. We had stopped the enemy's Tet Offensive in its tracks, and now we had him on the run. At least that was what we thought.

The next day, 1 April, Charlie Company moved by CH-47 Chinook helicopters to FSB Bolt, about ten kilometers south of Tay Ninh City. That same day we conducted a combat assault into an LZ west of the Van Dong River just four kilometers from the border with Cambodia. Three Warrior rifle companies landed on the same LZ. Charlie Company made the first landing in UH-1s and secured the LZ for Alpha and Delta companies, which landed in CH-47s. There was no sign of any enemy activity.

We had been briefed that the whole area was a "free-fire zone," which meant that we could shoot at anything that moved. The Vietnamese district chief had ensured Brigadier General Forbes that all the friendlies had been resettled closer to Tay Ninh.

Because it was late in the day when the final lift landed, we moved only a short distance before setting up an NDP. All three Warrior companies shared a portion of the perimeter. It was the dry season, so we dug our fighting positions in the dry rice paddies. There were a few Vietnamese hooches about three hundred meters from the perimeter, but our patrols reported them deserted.

Just before dark our FOs began to register DEFCONs around the perimeter. Each line company defended a sector of the perimeter. When our FO, Paul Lange, plotted our DEFCONs, I wasn't paying much attention. Consequently, I was caught by surprise when the first white phosphorus (WP) marking round detonated directly over our heads just as I finished off a can of C rations. No one was hurt, but I went off on Lange. I told him if that was the best he could do, he would probably get us all killed.

At dusk, we spotted three VC in black pajamas as they ran toward a hut about three hundred meters from our company's sector of the perimeter. They carried a mortar tube and base plate. I ordered my 90mm recoilless rifle team to fire on the house. The weapon had not been properly boresighted, and the rounds missed their target. Next I called for mortar fire on the hut. The first round landed about twenty meters beyond the house, and the next round fell just in front of the house. The target was bracketed, so the mortar men fired for effect. The barrage obliterated the hooch, and the ground shook with a secondary explosion as mortar rounds stored inside the hut detonated. After that, I was pretty sure we weren't going to be mortared that night. Nonetheless, everyone remained on edge.

Just after midnight, we spotted what we thought were truck headlights in the direction of the border. Concerned that the NVA may be trucking troops right up to the border for an attack on our position, I ordered Lieutenant Lange to call in an artillery fire mission. When the target coordinates were passed to the artillery fire direction center at FSB Bolt, they refused to fire the mission. The targets were inside Cambodia. "Fuck it," I responded when Lange gave me the news. "You artillery pukes make me sick." That was unfair on my part, but I was beginning to really dislike this war.

We moved out at dawn. Each company moved separately in a northeasterly direction. We started finding a few hooches with sizeable stores of rice. No inhabitants were around anywhere. We dumped the rice on the ground and tried to make it inedible by pissing on it and tossing smoke grenades on it. Then we saw columns of smoke off to the east. The other Warrior companies were torching the hooches in their path. When First Sergeant Holmes produced a Zippo lighter and lit the thatch roof on a hooch, I didn't object.

We were preparing to move out when I heard General Forbes on the battalion radio net chewing out our battalion commander.

"What is going on, Warrior Six? What's all that smoke?" Forbes was bearing down on our area in his C&C ship. Mastoris, in his own C&C ship, was orbiting over Delta Company.

"If I see another hooch being burned, I'm going to court-martial you and your company commanders!" Forbes threatened.

That put a halt to our scorched-earth tactics. Mastoris chewed our asses on the radio and clarified the rules of engagement. Later that day we found another cache of about three hundred pounds of rice and some documents. We also detained an old man who had apparently been left behind by his family. We had him flown out to the fire support base. The next day we found an unoccupied enemy base camp. The NVA and VC were staying out of sight, possibly across the border.

The following day, 4 April, we conducted an airmobile

assault into an LZ about fifteen kilometers to the northwest in an area called the Straight Edge Woods. The western edge of the woods, which encompassed several grid squares on our topographical maps, was perfectly straight, giving the area its name.

A four-man brigade LRRP team was on the same lift as Charlie Company. I wasn't briefed on their mission, but I assumed they would go their own way once we landed. As the slicks descended to treetop level, I noticed that the whole LZ was covered with giant ant hills. We used them as cover as we maneuvered off the LZ. The LZ was cold, so we secured it and waited for the Alpha and Delta company insertions.

As soon as the other companies had landed, we began our movement into the Straight Edge Woods. I noticed the LRRPs were following my rear platoon. At the time I didn't give it much thought, figuring they would move off toward their own objective at some point. We pushed into the woods for a couple of clicks and linked up with Delta and Alpha companies in a large rectangular clearing.

Lieutenant Colonel Mastoris flew in to our location and instructed us to set up an NDP around the edge of the clearing. As we were digging in, I received a radio call from the deputy brigade commander, Col. Fred Davison, who was trying to locate our LZ. He couldn't raise anyone on the battalion radio net, so he called in on my company frequency to ask if I could direct his pilot to our LZ. I looked up and caught sight of his OH-23 light observation helicopter several miles to our southwest heading straight toward Cambodia.

"Redcatcher Five, this is Marauder Six. I've got you in sight. We're at your six o'clock position, popping smoke. Make a one-eighty turn; you're off course."

The helicopter went into a tight turn and circled back to our LZ. That pilot needs a lesson in map reading, I thought.

Colonel Davison walked our perimeter and talked to some of the men before he lifted off. While he was on the ground, one of the Charlie Company grunts, who was listening to AFN radio news on a transistor radio, heard that Dr. Martin Luther King Jr. had been assassinated in Memphis. Colonel Davison was African-American, and the news made a heartfelt impression on him as it did on all of us. We all pondered about events back in the States. It added to our worries. While I didn't notice it immediately, I think Charlie Company was never quite the same after that day. News of riots in Washington, New York, Chicago, and Detroit reached us in the days that followed Dr. King's death. The whole country seemed to be at war with itself. Blacks against whites, generation against generation, and government against the protesters. As soldiers, we continued to fight and die together, but we were never as cohesive as before.

After Colonel Davison lifted off, we settled in for the night. The LRRP team was still in the perimeter, digging in near my CP. Their sergeant was on the radio, calling in his location for the night. Personally, I didn't give a damn about the LRRPs spending the night within our perimeter, but I was curious about their mission. When I heard the sergeant calling in his map coordinates I checked them on my map. I noticed that these coordinates were for a location about a kilometer to our south. Apparently, the team leader was calling in a false location. I walked over and asked, "Sergeant, do you know how to read a map?"

"Yes . . . Sir," he responded.

"Then why did you just call in the wrong location to your platoon leader?"

"Well . . . er, you know, Sir, we're only a couple of kilometers from the Cambodian border, and, er, Sir, we don't know this area at all. I thought we'd stay here tonight with you and move out in the morning."

"Okay, but let's get your platoon leader back on the radio. I want to talk to him."

I updated the LRRP platoon leader on his team leader's

deception, and we agreed that it was too late to send the team out into the bush. It was agreed that the LRRPs would move out at dawn.

The night passed quietly, but all hell broke loose the following morning. It started just after Mastoris's C&C ship touched down on the north side of the LZ. Mastoris, his RTOs, and the artillery liaison officer jumped out, and the Huey began to lift off. When the UH-1 was about twenty feet off the ground, the enemy started mortaring the LZ. Mortar rounds burst under the skids as the ship lifted off. Miraculously, the C&C ship cleared the LZ and flew off.

The mortar attack continued. Most of the rounds now fell on the northwest side of the perimeter, where Charlie Company was tied in with Alpha Company. Machine-gun fire from the jungle opened up on us. Then a mortar round scored a direct hit on an Alpha Company foxhole, killing two sergeants. Three soldiers next to my CP were wounded.

First Sergeant Holmes and I were checking Charlie Company's positions not more than twenty meters away when the attack started. We both dove into the nearest hole. It was the FO's foxhole. We jumped in on top of Lieutenant Lange and Sergeant Hapgood. I told Lange to give me his radio handset so I could call in a fire mission to silence the enemy machine gunner who was zeroing in on our position. The only problem was that the radio was at the bottom of the hole underneath our four bodies. After a lot of cursing, I was finally able to retrieve the handset, and I called in a fire mission to a 155mm howitzer battery at FSB Bolt. We were out of range of our own 105mm direct-support battery from 2/40th Artillery. Moments later the 155 rounds were tearing up the jungle northwest of the LZ. We were still taking sporadic mortar rounds, so I told Lange to keep shifting the 155 rounds. Then I dashed back to my own CP. Charlie Company grunts blazed away into the jungle to their front.

When I reached my CP foxhole, Kaylor said that the LRRP team sergeant was calling over the battalion net, saying that he had spotted about a hundred NVA moving close to his position. The LRRP team had left the perimeter as instructed at dawn and was now about five hundred meters south of the LZ. The battalion artillery liaison officer shifted the 155s and asked the LRRP sergeant to adjust these fires. The team leader said he couldn't; he and his team were hiding in a bomb crater and the NVA were all around them. The sergeant called for gunships and an extraction ship. A team of gunships was already en route to the LZ to try to find the mortars that were shelling us. They were diverted to the LRRP location, where they engaged the NVA with miniguns and rockets. Under the covering fire provided by the gunships, the LRRPs were able to scramble to a tiny one-ship LZ from which they were extracted. By then we had stopped receiving incoming mortar and machine-gun fire at the LZ.

Mastoris called for his C&C bird and ordered us to move north to search the area in which we thought the enemy mortars were located. The gunships reported a body count of twelve NVA near the LRRP position, but they couldn't locate any more enemy south of the LZ; they had melted away into the dense jungle.

We moved northwest out of the LZ but left a squad-size stay-behind patrol to keep the LZ under surveillance. About thirty minutes after we left, an NVA squad began searching our abandoned positions on the LZ, scrounging for C rations and other discarded items. The stay-behind patrol opened up on the NVA squad and killed one in a short but violent firefight. The other NVA ran into the jungle, dragging their wounded with them.

The Warrior battalion continued operations in the Straight Edge Woods area for another three days. We maneuvered as separate companies but always remained close enough to reinforce each other. The weather remained oppressively hot and dry.

We had a team from the 49th Scout Dog Platoon attached to our company during this phase of the operation. The Charlie Company grunts ensured that the handler had enough water for the dog, but one afternoon while moving through a chest-high field of elephant grass, the dog expired from the heat and lack of air. The dog handler and the grunts took it hard.

On 9 April, the 199th Infantry Brigade's participation in Operation Wilderness ended. The Warrior battalion losses were light, and no significant contact was made on the operation. Nevertheless, we confiscated more than three thousand pounds of rice.

The same afternoon that the operation ended, my officers and I were unwinding a bit at the CP over a couple of beers. I mentioned in passing how dissatisfied I was with the artillery support during the operation, and I chided Paul Lange, my FO, about his performance. We started to banter back and forth. It seemed harmless at first, but soon got serious. I liked Lange, but he didn't always follow orders well and had a big mouth. He also knew how to push my buttons. Words escalated to finger pointing and shoving, and before either of us knew it, we were both out of control. First Sergeant Holmes jumped in and separated us as the platoon leaders looked on in disbelief. At that moment I knew Lange had to go. I told him to pack his gear and get out of my CP. Then I radioed his battery commander and arranged to swap FOs with Alpha Company. Paul Lange and I both lost it that day near Tay Ninh, but both of us made a career in the Army and remain good friends today.

On 10 April, while we were awaiting orders for our next operation, a wasp stung me, and I had to be medevaced to the battalion aid station. I had a reaction, and the medics were concerned that I might go into anaphylactic shock.

After passing an uncomfortable night, I returned to the company in the morning. I had to get back because we had been ordered to move overland by trucks to our main base camp at Long Binh.

Our route was hazardous. We were to meet our transport just south of Tay Ninh and drive southeast on Highway 22 toward Saigon. The road was known as Ambush Alley in 1968. It wound its way south to Go Dau Ha, where the convoy would pick up Highway 1, follow that, pass through Cu Chi, and move on past Hoc Mon until reaching the Saigon area. After passing through the city, it was another fifteen miles to our base camp in Long Binh.

It was midafternoon before the convoy was ready to move out. Delta Troop, 17th Armored Cavalry, provided security. We were promised on-station gunship support until we reached Saigon. I decided to mount one of my rifle platoons and my own CP group on the ACAVs.

We moved out in the lead of the convoy and raced through the shadowy rubber plantations just south of Tay Ninh at full throttle. Burned-out tank and APC hulks, battle debris from recent fights in this area, lay beside the highway. The ACAV commanders kept their .50-caliber machine guns trained on tree lines along both sides of the road. We all rode on top of the tracks. If a vehicle hit a mine, it was better to be blown off than be trapped inside.

I breathed easier when we drove past Go Dau Ha. We'd been lucky; our rapid movement caught the enemy by surprise. We made it through Ambush Alley unscathed.

We rolled into the outskirts of Saigon about 1800 hours. The Vietnamese civilian and military police must have known we were coming. Two jeep-loads of MPs picked up the convoy at the edge of the city and escorted us through with traffic sirens blaring. We didn't even slow down. Our police escort, guns drawn, cleared a path through the stream of aged black Citroëns, small blue-and-yellow Renault taxicabs, and dilapidated buses. The drivers in our convoy were alternately braking and accelerating, trying to avoid the three-wheeled Lambrettas and motor scooters that darted recklessly into our path. White-gloved national police ("White Mice") stationed at the major intersections waved us through the snarl of traffic. As we rolled into the heart of the city, the streets were packed with people moving in all directions—diminutive Vietnamese men in white shirts, slacks, and sandals, their women in black slacks and white *ao dai*. Gaudy neon signs pointed the way to bars, and we could hear the jangle of Western rock music through their open doors. Painted Vietnamese bar girls waited in seductive poses in the doorways to lure khaki-clad MACV GIs into the bars and nightclubs. Our route took us past the famed Continental Palace Hotel as its terrace was filling up with the regular nightly clientele of rich Vietnamese, members of the international press corps, and Americans from the embassy. The civilians paid little attention to our convoy as they sipped their cognac. Military convoys passing through the city were commonplace in 1968.

Charlie Company's war-weary grunts stared with fascination at the alluring sights of the city. They were so far removed from this side of the war that they couldn't process the images that were flashing before their eyes.

We crossed the Saigon River and drove northward, passing through a broad expanse of dry rice paddy fields on the final leg of our journey. The convoy took a few sniper rounds while crossing a bridge near Thu Duc, but no one was hit, and we rolled safely into Camp Frenzell-Jones in the warm tropical night.

chapter eleven
along the song dong nai

> April is the cruellest month, breeding
> Lilacs out of the dead land.
> —T. S. ELIOT,
> "The Waste Land"

April 1968

As usual, our stand-down at Camp Frenzell-Jones was brief. We had only one day to replenish our supplies, issue clean jungle fatigues to the troops, and give everyone a chance to visit the PX and enlisted club. There was not enough time for the exhausted troops to recuperate.

The frenzied pace of the Warrior battalion's operations over the past two months was taking its toll. The grunts in the line companies lived out of their rucksacks for weeks on end, subsisted mainly on C rations, were constantly on the move during the day, and on ambush or alert at night. They rarely had the opportunity to bathe, and if they did, it was in a muddy stream or canal. The hardships wore us down after a while, and it was not unusual for an infantryman to lose twenty pounds or more after a few months in the field. Many also suffered from chronic diarrhea and jungle rot. While disease and illness wore down the body, stress and anxiety wore down the spirit. A one-day stand-down at the base camp often did more harm than good.

In fact, these brief sojourns only created more enmity between the grunts and the rear-echelon troops. The field soldiers got a snapshot view of the base camp lifestyle the support troops led, and they despised them for it. In contrast to the hardships that we endured, support troops had warm showers, freshly laundered and pressed uniforms every day, mess hall meals three times a day, and access to PX items such as stereo equipment, hard liquor, and cigarettes. They slept in barracks cleaned by Vietnamese house girls who shined their boots and, in some cases, even satisfied their sexual desires. When the men were off duty they had access to live entertainment and liquor at the air-conditioned clubs. Their whole day was ruined when a battalion of grunts came out of the bush to invade the base camp facilities. The grunts weren't impressed that the support troops put in long days repairing trucks, typing up paperwork, building barracks, and performing an endless number of other tasks. It didn't take more than a couple of beers and an off-hand remark to start a brawl.

On this stand-down, Colonel Davison invited me to eat dinner at the field grade officers mess. The tables in the mess were covered with white linen tablecloths and set with real china and flatware. A dining room orderly brought us a menu, which listed a variety of main courses. I chose steak and lobster and gulped down a glass of white wine. Dinner music played on the mess stereo system. I enjoyed the dinner and my conversation with Colonel Davison, but I felt strangely out of place in this setting. Rank has it privileges, but this was carrying it a bit too far. Doubts about the future of this war began to weigh heavily on my mind. Time didn't allow for too much contemplation, however.

The following day, 13 April, the Warrior battalion moved by CH-47 to FSB Farrell, located just south of the Dong Nai River in Long Khanh Province, about fifteen kilometers north of Highway 1. Nearby, the Dong Nai turns abruptly west from its southerly course through War Zone D. A large unworked rubber plantation lay southwest of FSB Farrell. The area to the west of the rubber plantation was dense jungle, but the area to the east was somewhat more open.

Charlie Company was to search and clear the rubber plantation. We moved two kilometers south into the rubber to reach the plantation's cantonment area. The place was deserted. About a dozen workers' barracks had badly damaged tile roofs. On a small hill overlooking the cantonment area was the abandoned plantation director's house surrounded by an eight-foot moss-covered brick-and-stucco wall with sentry posts at each corner. The walls of the compound and house were pock-marked with mortar shrapnel and bullet holes, and the whole compound was overgrown, slowly being reclaimed by the jungle. All furnishings had been removed from the house, and broken red tiles and glass littered the floors.

After we searched the buildings I decided to set up our night defensive position around the hilltop. The troops dug in outside the walls while the CP group set up beneath the shelter of the plantation house verandah.

It was a spooky place. As the setting sun cast long shadows down the rows of rubber trees, I thought of the hundreds of peasants who spent their lives collecting raw latex from the rubber trees. I once read an account about a coolie's life on one of these plantations. It was one step above slavery. The workers toiled from dawn to dusk each day collecting the raw latex in little tin cans, trying to make their daily quotas. When they weren't collecting, they were clearing brush from between the trees. It was a miserable life.

The night passed quietly. In the predawn darkness, I thought I heard the sound of a clamorous gong near the barracks huts, but perhaps it was only a dream. At first light, I hurriedly ate a C ration of ham slices and swallowed a mouthful of water from my canteen. I met with the platoon leaders at the CP and briefed them on the day's operation.

Charlie Company was to sweep westward through the plantation all the way to the jungle beyond. Two rifle platoons would be at the front and the third rifle platoon at the rear. The CP group and Mortar Platoon would move between the lead rifle platoons and the reserve platoon.

Moving through the rubber plantation was easy. The underbrush and weeds in the rubber groves had grown up some, but not much. The glossy-leafed rubber trees were planted in neat rows as far as the eye could see. Most of the trees still had small tin cups wedged into notches in their straight trunks to catch the milky latex that oozed from within the trunk. It was shady and cool under the trees.

After about an hour, I called a halt. We set up a perimeter around two intersecting dirt roads in the rubber grove. It was very quiet and peaceful. The sunlight that filtered through the glossy leaves was warming but not hot. The war seemed far away in the morning calm, but not for more than a few minutes.

The sharp *crack* of several AK-47s firing on full automatic shattered the air and kicked up dirt around us, and an RPG *swoosh*ed down the road from the west to detonate about thirty meters behind us.

Bob Stanley's 3d Platoon was directly to our front. Without hesitation, they returned fire with M60 machine guns and M16s. I ordered Howard Tuber's 1st Platoon to move to support Stanley. As far as I could tell, no one was hit.

We could see small groups of VC moving across the rows of rubber trees about 150 meters to our front. Based on the volume of AK-47 fire, it seemed like no more than a platoon-size force. Apparently, we took our rest break just short of their ambush site. No doubt they thought that we had detected their ambush position, and they opened fire prematurely.

I told my FO to call an artillery fire mission as the firefight continued. As I was trying to reposition an M60 machine gun to fire directly up the road, the FO informed me that the artillery fire direction officer turned down the fire mission. Artillery fire was restricted to prevent damage to the rubber trees owned by Michelin. I couldn't believe it. I grabbed the FO's radio handset and screamed, "Send me the fucking bill for the trees! Fuck Michelin, and fuck the French!"

We got our fire mission a few minutes later. Artillery rounds burst in the trees, raining shrapnel down upon the VC. They withdrew and headed for the nearby jungle, leaving behind a couple of field packs and some blood trails, but no bodies. We also found three Chi-Com Claymores tied to trees in front of their kill zone. God was with us that day. We took no casualties.

After our close call we moved out northwestward, following the blood trails left by the VC. The trail led us out of the rubber and into the jungle. We paralleled a well-worn jungle track. After about an hour we reached a place that had been hit by a B-52 strike several months earlier. Huge bomb craters pockmarked the whole area. The earth around the craters was scorched and littered with huge pieces of bomb shrapnel. Fallen trees, their trunks snapped like toothpicks, impeded our movement, as did the stumps of saplings and torn undergrowth. The few trees still standing were scarred by shrapnel hits, their branches burned and broken.

Then we entered an area that must have been an enemy overnight bivouac. The B-52s had found their target. Decomposed corpses, body parts, and scorched rucksacks were scattered throughout the area. One body was still lying in a jungle hammock. A piece of shrapnel had decapitated the man; we found his head lying on the ground several feet away. It was a morbid scene that has stayed with me forever.

Late that afternoon, during a halt, I had each platoon send out a cloverleaf patrol to ensure we weren't being followed. A grunt was moving through the brush when he suddenly came face-to-face with a VC. They were less than ten paces apart. The startled men fired simultaneously, missing each other by inches. Both men turned and took off running. We fired 60mm mortar rounds into the jungle where the VC fled.

Day's end found us in a clearing on the south bank of the Dong Nai River. Major Ed King, S-3, flew in to our location to update me on a change of mission. The 11th Armored Cavalry Regiment was moving south through War Zone D toward the river, and engineers were reconnoitering along the river for sites at which they could build a floating pontoon bridge for the cavalry to cross. Our battalion had the mission of securing the bridge site while the engineers built the bridge. King gave me a warning order to be prepared to move to the proposed site once the engineers completed their survey and decided where the bridge was to be built.

Later that night, one of our ambush patrols opened fire on four VC, killing one. The following morning a Charlie Company daylight patrol killed another VC near the river and recovered the VC's AK-47 and rucksack.

At midday I was ordered by Lieutenant Colonel Mastoris to start moving east along the river. The engineers had decided upon a bridge site about five kilometers to our east. The colonel also asked me for a favor: He needed a radio operator for the battalion TOC, and he wanted Cliff Kaylor, my battalion RTO.

There was no question that Kaylor was the best qualified for the job, but I hated to give him up. I relied heavily on Cliff, but his attitude about the war was getting under my skin. First Sergeant Holmes, who sensed the friction between Kaylor and me, weighed in on the matter. He told me that it was probably a good idea for Kaylor to leave Charlie

Company, arguing that Cliff spent seven months in the
bush and deserved a break. I finally agreed. First Sergeant
Holmes told Kaylor to pack his ruck and catch the next resupply bird headed for FSB Farrell. Neither Top nor I told
him about his new job. All we said was that he had to report to the battalion commander. Kaylor thought I had
brought him up on charges.

Before moving out, the TOC radioed us that a B-52 strike
was about to occur some ten kilometers north of our location. We couldn't hear the bombers because they were flying at high altitude, but we spotted the vapor trails. The
B-52s resembled tiny silver fish in the topaz blue sky. The
bombs began falling into the jungle. A ridgeline about a
kilometer north of the river hid the flash of the explosions,
but the ground beneath our feet shook from the force of the
concussions. Moments later we saw huge clouds of dust
and black smoke billowing up beyond the ridgeline.

It took another three days for the engineers to move the
bridging equipment to their site. In the interim, I was directed to search and clear the area along the south bank of
the river. On 17 April, a small group of VC walked into one
of our night ambush sites. The ambush patrol was still setting up their Claymores. The VC dropped their packs and
took off as the Charlie Company grunts opened fire. The
ambush patrol moved on to an alternate site.

The following morning Lieutenant Hinkley reported that
a gutsy VC had crept up to his perimeter during the night
and cut the firing wires and removed the electric blasting
caps from two Claymores. I asked Hinkley's men if they
heard any noise in front of their position. One of the grunts,
a new replacement, said he thought he heard something.

"Why didn't you fire your Claymores if you heard
noises?" I asked.

"Well, the VC sometimes turn the Claymores around so

the blast would have taken me out," the man answered. "Besides, I thought it was just an animal that I heard."

I was pissed off with this response, and told Hinkley that he needed to jack up the man's squad leader. The soldier should have tossed a frag to his front and killed the VC who was tampering with the Claymores. I was alarmed because this incident demonstrated that the VC could penetrate our perimeter at night. Moreover, I knew that the VC would use the electric blasting caps for their command-detonated mines or booby traps.

We reached the bridge site on 21 April. The engineer convoy rolled into the area shortly after our arrival. They brought with them every piece of float bridging equipment available in III Corps, along with bulldozers and scoop loaders. The earthmoving equipment operators went to work immediately, clearing the southern approach to the bridge.

Security for the engineer vehicles posed a problem. Our perimeter was about twice the size of a normal rifle company perimeter. We had to spread the vehicles out so they wouldn't present an easy target for a VC mortar or rocket attack. By nightfall Charlie Company was dug in along a crescent-shaped perimeter anchored on the river at each end.

The area on the north side of the river also had to be secured to protect the engineers while they worked. I coordinated with the engineer company commander to use some of his boats to ferry 1st Platoon to the northern bank. Tuber's men crossed in small boats under covering fire from M60 machine guns and mortars. The river was about 250 meters wide at this point. The 1st Platoon's landing was unopposed, and Tuber soon reported that he had secured the bridgehead. Then the bridge builders went to work.

It was interesting to watch the engineers maneuver the floating pontoons into position, secure them, and then start laying the ramp. The current was fairly swift, and progress was painstakingly slow. The engineers worked throughout the night, using searchlights to illuminate the bridge site. The illumination increased the risk of a mortar attack, but the engineers were on a tight time schedule. The 11th Armored Cavalry Regiment had to cross the river.

About 2300, a sampan skimmed around the bend in the river about a hundred meters from the bridge site. Two VC in black pajamas swiftly paddled the sampan toward the bank and disappeared into the jungle when they were taken under fire. The bridging work continued through the next morning.

About midmorning Holmes and I walked toward the work site. We saw two Vietnamese girls emerge from one of the engineer vans parked nearby. They were giggling as they walked past us toward a water trailer. I sent First Sergeant Holmes to investigate. When I returned to the company CP, Holmes wasn't there. When he showed up an hour later, he said, "Captain, those engineers have their stuff together."

"How's that, Top?"

"They bring their own whores along to service their troops."

"What!"

"Yep. They've got that van fitted out as a mobile whorehouse. I checked out the whole operation," Holmes continued.

"I'm sure you did, Top. I wondered what took you so long."

The engineers finished the bridge that evening. The next morning we were relieved of the security mission by a battalion from the 1st Infantry Division, the Big Red One.

I was glad to be leaving the bridge site. The bridge was bound to attract the enemy's attention sooner or later. As it turned out, the bridge site was mortared after we departed. The bridge itself was not damaged, but the engineers lost several vehicles and the 1st Infantry's battalion took some casualties. The 11th Armored Cavalry Regiment crossed a day later, moving on toward Long Binh and Saigon in time to help counter the enemy's May Offensive.

Charlie Company left the bridge site on the afternoon of 23 April, the same day as the student rebellion at Columbia University. We made an airmobile assault into an LZ about five kilometers north of Highway 1. The Warrior battalion headquarters moved into FSB Tri-Corners, near Trang Bom village on Highway 1. Our LZ was cold. Charlie Company's luck was holding.

I surveyed the area as we were inbound to the LZ. The area had been cleared of jungle, and a few Vietnamese hooches dotted the landscape. After the second lift landed, we began our sweep to the northwest. By late afternoon we reached some high ground on which we established an NDP. We had good fields of fire all around, but the ground was rocky and it was difficult to dig foxholes. Our entrenching tools were about useless; the best the men could do was scrape shallow prone positions in the hard ground. It was too late in the day to move to another location.

I wasn't worried about a ground attack on the perimeter. We had good observation and fields of fire. With artillery and mortar support, along with our own company interlocking fires, we would decimate an enemy ground assault before it got within a hundred meters of the perimeter. On the other hand, I was concerned about a possible VC mortar attack.

The company CP was set up on the topographical crest of the hill. This was another mistake on my part, but there was a crude thatched hut on the crest, so we moved in. Beneath a sleeping platform in the hut was a shallow dug-out area about twelve inches deep.

I walked the perimeter before dark, visiting each platoon's sector. The men had done their best to fortify their positions with the few sandbags that each of them carried. Jaynes said he had tried to stabilize the mortar base-plates, but he wasn't confident that his crews could put out any accurate fire.

Just after midnight, we heard the tell-tale *thunk* of rounds as they hit the firing pins of the VC mortar tubes. The mortar rounds were in the air! I scrambled off the sleeping platform and crawled into the shallow depression, burying my face in the dirt. The rest of the CP group scattered. My RTOs lay on the ground outside the hut.

The first mortar rounds landed short of the perimeter. I heard more mortar rounds being dropped down the tubes. This time the rounds impacted inside the perimeter. The VC mortar crew was walking the mortar rounds up the hill. Suddenly it dawned on me that the hooch was probably the target for VC gunners. I ran outside and hit the dirt next to my RTOs. Three mortar rounds slammed into the ground about thirty feet away, but none of us was hit. Clods of dirt splattered our backs and steel helmets, and my ears rang for several minutes after the blasts.

It was over as quickly as it started. Fewer than a dozen rounds were fired on our position. I called for artillery fire on the suspected location of the enemy mortar, but the VC mortar crew was no doubt hauling ass by then. Specialist John Hedlin of 1st Platoon and one other soldier were hit, but their wounds were not serious enough to call a night dust-off. The next morning I found the tail fin from one of the 82mm mortar rounds that landed near us. I kept it as a reminder never to set up in an area where we couldn't dig in properly.

The next day, the Warrior S-3, Maj. Ed King, flew into our position with some sad news. Our sister battalion, 3/7th Infantry (the "Cottonbalers"), had run into an enemy base camp the day before. Eight men, including the company commander, Capt. John South, were killed in the ensuing fight. South was one of the best and most highly respected company commanders in the 199th Brigade. I knew him only slightly, but the news still came as a shock. Dozens more Cottonbalers were wounded, including Capt. Tony Smalldone, another superb company commander in the 3/7th Infantry. King also gave us our marching orders for the day.

We moved northwest into the jungle. The area was crisscrossed with trails, so we moved slowly and sent out small recon patrols to our front and flanks. At night we formed tight perimeters and dug in. Usually, we sent out three ambush patrols on trails leading toward our perimeter. The VC, however, were keeping their distance.

On 26 April, we made contact with a small VC force that fired a few rounds at our point element before melting into the jungle. Staff Sergeant Donald William, a squad leader in 1st Platoon, had a narrow escape. An AK round struck the side of his helmet just above the camouflage band and penetrated the steel at a glancing angle. The spent round then spun through the gap between the steel pot and the helmet liner, knocking the helmet from the sergeant's head. It gave him a terrific headache, but that was all. William showed me his helmet after the fight. That incident made all of us believers in the steel helmet. Never again would I let my men wear bush hats in lieu of the battle-tested steel pot.

On 30 April, Mastoris flew into our position and dropped off a reporter. Carl Schoettler of the *Baltimore Evening Sun* accompanied us that day as we moved westward to an LZ about five kilometers away. I wasn't keen about having a reporter tag along on a combat operation, but Schoettler turned out to be an OK guy. He established instant rapport with grunts, and he reminded me of what Ernie Pyle must have been like. Schoettler wrote an article about Charlie Company and 3d Platoon medic Pfc. David Loughrie, of Cumberland, Maryland, that was published in the *Sun*.

* * *

We set up a company patrol base near the LZ that Mastoris directed us to. The men were worn out. The daily grind of hacking through several kilometers of jungle took its toll on the men. The monsoon season was beginning, too. We were experiencing rainfall every two or three days. It would rain for about an hour in a deluge. We could hear it as it hit the jungle canopy above our heads, then we would wait a couple of minutes for it to penetrate and soak us to the bone. Jungle rot was becoming a problem, and the men were becoming used to checking out each other for leeches two or three times a day.

We were going to be operating out of the same company base for several days, so we constructed fighting bunkers with overhead cover built from logs we cut in the surrounding jungle. We laid the logs over the tops of bunkers and covered them with three layers of sandbags. Each bunker had interlocking fires with the bunkers on the left and right. The 81mm mortars were placed in sandbagged firing pits.

When they were not working on improving their bunkers, the troops patrolled the surrounding jungle. We sent out night ambush patrols to surprise any enemy moving in the area. There weren't going to be any surprise attacks on Charlie Company while we were in this static position.

Lieutenant Colonel Mastoris sent out Maj. Frank Gillespie to spend the day with Charlie Company. He was scheduled to replace Ed King, the Warrior S-3. King was a superb tactician and had always been up front with the Warrior company commanders. When he thought we were right, he was our advocate with the other battalion and brigade staff officers. However, when we overstepped our bounds, he was not shy about chewing our asses out. His shoes were going to be hard to fill.

Gillespie was a West Pointer and had served a previous tour with the 1st Cavalry Division. I didn't feel comfortable talking to him. He seemed uninterested in what I had to say. I was concerned. The 199th Brigade wasn't the 1st Cavalry. We didn't have the air assets or the ARA (aerial rocket artillery) that the 1st Cavalry had at its disposal. I had a feeling that the days ahead were going to be more difficult.

Around the first of May, we began receiving intelligence reports from the battalion S-2 that indicated another big enemy offensive was on the wind. One report was taken quite seriously by the intelligence people: A captured Vietcong colonel revealed that another nationwide offensive was scheduled to take place in early May. I didn't like this news one bit. My five-day R&R to Bangkok was scheduled for the week of 14 May, two weeks away. I had been in Vietnam for seven months, and in command of Charlie Company for four months, and I was looking forward to a break for a few days. Now the enemy was probably going to ruin that for me. I hoped that it was just another rumor, but it wasn't. May 1968 was to be the bloodiest month of the Vietnam War.

chapter twelve
the may offensive

For what can war, but endless war still breed?
—JOHN MILTON,
"On the Lord General Fairfax at the
Siege of Colchester"

The May Offensive 1968: Dai Do

On the night of 4 May, a taxi filled with more than a hundred pounds of TNT exploded outside the Saigon radio and TV station. This marked the beginning of the May Offensive in the Saigon area. More than thirty 122mm rockets and mortar rounds also hit the capital that night.

Although the Warrior battalion was deployed in the area east of Xuan Loc, we were caught up in the early hours of the offensive. At 0300 the battalion's FSB Tri-Corners came under mortar and 122mm rocket attack. We received a radio report that three VC battalions had crossed Highway 1 from north to south in our AO. Bien Hoa Air Base also was under rocket attack. For all that, it remained quiet in Charlie Company's sector. Nonetheless, I had the feeling that all that was about to change.

About 0700 on the morning of 5 May, the S-3 alerted me to have Charlie Company prepared to move within two hours to the Saigon area. We began dismantling the patrol base and packing our gear for the airmobile move. A few minutes later we were informed that the 1st Australian Task Force would relieve us of our mission in Long Khanh Province and that we would have to wait on its arrival before we moved.

142

An Aussie battalion landed by CH-47 Chinook helicopters on our LZ at about 0930. Although the Australians were new in-country, they were very professional. They moved rapidly off the LZ into positions in the surrounding jungle. I spoke to their battalion commander and oriented him on the surrounding terrain while First Sergeant Holmes grabbed the Aussie sergeant major for a quick conference. The pair took off for the LZ, then Top returned a few minutes later with a grin on his face and a case of Aussie beer under his arm.

As soon as the Aussies deployed their men, I had my platoon leaders line up their men in stick order for an airmobile extraction. We were allocated ten Hueys and one Chinook for the move. All we knew was that Charlie Company was going to airmobile into an area a few miles southwest of Saigon and provide security for the battalion's new fire base, Stephanie. Before our lift ships arrived, we received an intelligence report that the VC had launched an attack on Newport Bridge and were setting up antiaircraft installations around the Phu Tho Racetrack. I hoped that our helo pilots had the same information. It sounded like Tet all over again.

It was midafternoon before we lifted off the LZ. We flew southwest, crossing Highway 1 near Trang Bom. As the flight continued, the countryside below us changed from jungle to swamps and rice paddies interwoven with canals and meandering muddy streams. The rainy season was just beginning, so the paddies were not yet flooded. The Hueys stayed in a tight trail formation as they flew to the east of Saigon. Small villages and hamlets surrounded by groves of palm trees and banana trees dotted the landscape below.

Sitting in the right door of the lead UH-1, I had a good view of the city. A network of streams and canals surrounded the entire metropolitan area.

We skirted the city's port. Several ocean freighters were offloading their cargoes after having navigated the fifty

4/12th Infantry Fire Support Base Stephanie, May to June 1968

South Vietnam
Binh Tri Dong

to Saigon

Binh Tri Dong

palm grove

rice paddies

rice paddies

rice paddies

1st Platoon CP

2nd Platoon CP

artillery area

C/4-12 CP

B-TOC

mortar area

3rd Platoon CP

resupply pad

H

aid station

N

Diagram not to scale

miles of circuitous channel from the coast. Hundreds of barges and sampans plied their way up and down canals leading into the river's main channel. Many of these smaller watercraft were used to smuggle weapons, ammunition, and other contraband for the VC. Despite the fact that fighting was breaking out in some areas of Saigon, heavy traffic still flowed in and out of the sprawling city. I spotted the Y Bridge. It was still intact, and an assortment of trucks, taxis, and other vehicles were jammed bumper to bumper waiting to cross. It would have been impossible to completely cordon off the city to protect the mass of humanity and commerce from attack from the countryside.

Our flight continued, cutting across the southern tip of the Chinese district of Cholon. I spotted the Phu Tho Racetrack in the distance and was relieved that we weren't assaulting into that hotspot.

As we cleared the southwest tip of Cholon, the flight banked sharply to the right to take up a northerly heading. Our LZ was in the rice paddies about three miles southwest of Tan Son Nhut Air Base. The village of Binh Tri Dong lay about seven hundred meters south of the LZ.

Delta Company had already landed and secured the LZ. The plan called for Charlie Company to move south and occupy a cemetery a couple hundred meters from the village. This cemetery was surrounded by rice paddies, and a dirt road ran south from it and into the village. FSB Stephanie would be built right on top of this cemetery. Because the rainy season was beginning, it was the only dry ground available. Nonetheless, it sounded like bad karma to me!

I spoke with Jim Dabney, the Company D commander, while I waited for the CH-47 lift to arrive. A bank of dark, menacing clouds formed on the eastern horizon, a precursor to an hourlong torrential afternoon downpour. Both of us thought that our companies would be in action soon.

Once the CH-47 landed with the remainder of Charlie Company, Delta Company began to move out. Dabney and his men were heading due north for a kilometer, toward an area where stands of coconut palms and wild banana trees grew. I wished Jim good hunting.

The remainder of the battalion began to arrive later that afternoon. Alpha Company, led by Capt. Bob Reynolds, airmobiled into an LZ east of the new fire base while Capt. Lee Smith led Bravo Company into a position south of the village of Binh Tri Dong. A truck convoy escorted by ACAVs from Delta Troop, 17th Cavalry, was on the way from Long Binh.

We moved into the cemetery. The gravestones in some of the family plots were large monuments with Annamese inscriptions. I was surprised how soft and damp the ground was. A musty odor permeated the whole area.

A liaison officer from 2/40th Artillery arrived to mark firing positions for Charlie Battery's 105mm howitzers. I walked off a defensive perimeter with my platoon leaders. Howard Tuber's 1st Platoon would defend the northern portion of the fire base, Mike Hinkley's 2d Platoon would tie in with 1st Platoon and defend the eastern and part of the southern portion of the perimeter, and Bob Stanley's 3d Platoon would share the defense of the southern perimeter and also defend the western side of the fire base. By this time, all three lieutenants were seasoned platoon leaders, and I knew I could count on them.

We started to dig in, trying to avoid the numerous graves. As soon as fortification materials arrived we would begin to construct sandbagged bunkers with overhead cover. The fire-base bunkers were built from wooden 105mm howitzer and 81mm mortar ammo boxes filled with dirt, and steel culvert halves were added for overhead cover. Once each structure was built, it was covered with multiple layers of sandbags.

The artillery began arriving as Charlie Company was digging in around the perimeter. The 105mm howitzers, slung beneath CH-47s along with boxes of howitzer rounds, were lowered near the surveyed firing positions. The rotor wash of the hovering CH-47s kicked up swirling clouds of dust. Artillerymen quickly manhandled the howitzers into firing positions while other members of the crews placed red-and-white aiming stakes in front of each position.

After dropping the artillery, the CH-47s returned about forty minutes later with coiled rolls of concertina wire, steel engineer stakes, and bundles of sandbags. We began stringing the concertina wire around the perimeter and positioning Claymore mines in front of the wire.

The truck convoy from Long Binh arrived just before dusk. It was still drizzling. The heavy trucks and ACAVs soon turned the dirt road from the village into a morass of mud.

I showed the cavalry platoon leader where to position his ACAV along the perimeter. The ACAV .50-caliber and M60 machine guns added a significant amount of firepower to the perimeter. Two M42 Dusters (twin 40mm antiaircraft guns mounted on a tank chassis) also arrived with the convoy. These guns were used for direct ground fire and were quite effective in breaking up enemy ground attacks. I moved the Dusters into positions on the north side of the perimeter because I expected any attack to come from that direction.

A 155mm howitzer battery from II Field Force, Battery C, 2/35th Artillery, was in the convoy along with a number of battalion supply vehicles. The mud-spattered trucks and tracked vehicles rolled across the cemetery, carelessly knocking over ancient Vietnamese tombstones. One heavy truck had its front-right wheel sunk up to the axle in the soft mud of a freshly dug grave. We weren't winning any hearts and minds among the villagers by desecrating this sacred ground, but it wasn't my call.

The Charlie Company CP was set up a few yards behind the northern perimeter in 1st Platoon's sector. The battalion command group set up the TOC in two sandbagged Conex containers located in the center of the fire support base. More CH-47 sorties set down on the fire base even as darkness fell; their rotors created windstorms on the ground, blowing away unfilled sandbags and poncho shelters.

Under the cover of darkness, each rifle platoon set out night LPs some five hundred meters outside the perimeter. We could see the lights of the city to our east. The village to our south was dark. I had the feeling that it wasn't going to be a quiet night. Dinner was a cold C ration meal. After that I threw my bedroll down atop a grave and took a nap. My sleep was fitful, and I was haunted by spirits guarding this consecrated ground.

Bob Archibald shook me awake at 2130. Delta Company was in contact to our north. They reported that one of their LPs had killed one NVA and captured two prisoners. A few minutes later we watched a salvo of 122mm rockets arch over the northern horizon toward Tan Son Nhut Air Base. Shortly after midnight Delta company reported another contact with a squad of NVA soldiers north of FSB Stephanie.

I ordered Charlie Company to full alert. There was a grove of palm trees about four hundred meters north of the FSB that concerned me. It was in an area between Delta Company's position and the base. Jim Dabney could have some of his men in that area, I thought, but I didn't want to break radio silence to find out. We would sort it out in the morning. Meanwhile, I told Tuber to keep an eye on the area with his Starlight Scopes.

Around 0600 the following morning, Tuber's men spotted troops moving in the palm grove to our north. I ordered him to send out a squad-size patrol to check it out. I radioed Jim Dabney, and he cautioned me that the troops we spotted could have been one of his patrols.

Tuber's patrol was about fifty meters from the palm grove when they were taken under fire by an NVA squad. An RPD machine gun and a half-dozen AK-47s opened up on the squad. Private First Class Dennis Dunsing, a quiet Californian who was walking point, was mortally wounded. Private First Class Charles Ritter also caught a burst from the NVA, but his wounds were not fatal. The squad withdrew, carrying their dead and wounded man under covering fire from the perimeter.

First Sergeant Holmes and I ran to Tuber's platoon CP as soon as we saw what was happening. I told Tuber to have two more squads saddle up for an attack on the palm grove. Two tracks from D/17th Cavalry would support the attack. We moved out a few minutes later.

As we approached the palm grove, the NVA opened up on us with machine guns and AK-47s. We hit the dirt. The ACAVs returned fire with their .50-calibers as we crawled forward to close with the enemy.

As we got close enough to use hand grenades, I spotted an enemy foxhole about ten meters to my front in the palm grove. I pulled a grenade from my web gear and was about to pull the pin when two NVA suddenly stood up with their hands in the air. I had never been this close to NVA regulars. The two NVA were dressed in khaki uniforms with green canvas web gear, including ammo pouches. They wore pith helmets, and I noted that their hair was closely cropped. Fear was apparent in their eyes. I fought an impulse to finish them off. I couldn't do it. They looked like they were about fifteen years old and very frightened. I set the grenade on the ground and motioned them out of the hole with my CAR15. Top grabbed their machine gun while keeping his shotgun leveled at their midsections, and Archie searched them for hidden grenades and weapons.

Tuber's men, supported by some reinforcements from

Dabney's Company D, began to mop up the rest of the NVA in the palm grove. Top took charge of our prisoners and lowered the barrel of his shotgun as he started walking them back to the FSB. Bob Archibald and I rejoined the fight. We crawled forward to another fighting position, where we found a terribly wounded NVA soldier. This one was much older than our two prisoners. He couldn't move, so I called an ACAV forward and we lifted the man onto the ramp of the vehicle for evacuation. He died before the track reached the FSB. A total of nine NVA died in the fight, and we captured two. The prisoners were identified as members of the 267th NVA Battalion.

On my return to the fire base perimeter I went to the aid station to check on my wounded man; he had already been dusted off to the 3d Field Hospital in Saigon.

The fight had drained me. I remained despondent for the rest of the day. Father Angelo Liteky, the brigade Catholic chaplain, came by the company CP to talk with me. We shared a beer, but I wasn't in the mood to talk, so I asked him to go talk with the guys in 1st Platoon.

Delta Company had several firefights with squad-size NVA units later that morning and on into the afternoon, killing several and capturing a number of individual and crew-served weapons, including three 60mm mortars. Their own losses were two dead and seven wounded.

By early afternoon the FSB was taking small-arms fire from the village just to our south. The howitzer crewmen, who were still constructing sandbag parapets around their guns, were prime targets for the snipers. A soldier from battalion headquarters was also killed by a sniper, and another was wounded. It just wasn't safe to walk around the FSB. We needed a dirt berm around the whole thing, but the engineers didn't have a bulldozer available. In an attempt to silence the sniper fire coming from the village, the Charlie Battery commander moved one of his howitzers to the south side of the perimeter and began firing directly into the suspected sniper positions in the village. The howitzer blew away house after house until the sniper fire subsided. Fires still burned in the village as a striated tropical sunset gave way to the blackness of the night.

Shortly after dark, Charlie Company's line platoons set out their LPs. Three men in each platoon were assigned to this mission. Just before 2100, the 3d Platoon LP on the south side of the perimeter reported movement to its front. NVA snipers, using the paddy dikes as cover, were moving in closer to the fire base's perimeter. The LP's M79 grenadier fired a few rounds, and the enemy soldiers withdrew back toward the village.

By 2200 hours Delta Company was springing ambushes throughout their AO north of the FSB.

I was still concerned with that palm grove north of the perimeter. Tuber's platoon had sent out an LP to that area. At 2300, Tuber's men on the perimeter were staring through their Starlight Scopes when they spotted seven NVA soldiers moving along a road that led toward the palm grove. The 1st Platoon had lost radio contact with its LP. Apparently, the LP had gone to ground, or the troops were asleep. About an hour and a half later another group of about twenty NVA soldiers was spotted as it moved in the direction of the LP's position. We couldn't fire on them for fear of wiping out our own LP. I ran to Tuber's platoon CP to get an update. Tuber was on the radio trying to make contact with the LP; he wanted the men to withdraw to the perimeter, but they were not answering his radio call.

Lieutenant Tuber, who cared deeply for his men, was near frantic.

"I'm going out there to get those men," he said.

"Let's wait a few minutes and see what happens," I cautioned him.

"No, I'm going right now." There was no stopping him.

"All right damn it, I'll go with you."

Our decision violated every principle in the book, but our emotions were running high. Carrying only our CAR15s, we slipped through the concertina wire and moved in a low crouch from paddy dike to paddy dike toward the tree line. Suddenly, we heard muffled voices coming from the perimeter, trying to get our attention.

"Come back, come back!" So far, we hadn't spotted any enemy, but the men on the perimeter had Starlight Scopes trained on the tree line.

We retraced our steps back to the perimeter. Norman Powell, Tuber's platoon sergeant, met us at the wire. He told us that he had spotted a platoon-size NVA patrol moving toward the palm grove. About a half-hour later, Tuber made radio contact with his LP. They reported that the NVA platoon walked right past their position in the darkness. Tuber instructed the LP to sit tight until daylight.

A few minutes after Tuber and I reentered the perimeter, both Delta Company and Alpha Company came under heavy attack by the NVA. Delta Company was hit the hardest. The fire base's 105mm and 155mm howitzers opened fire in support of the two companies, as did the battalion 4.2-inch mortar platoon. From the perimeter, we watched the exchange of red and green tracers that marked both firefights. Jim Dabney radioed that his position was being assaulted by two to three hundred NVA, while Bob Reynolds, the Company A commander, estimated that he was in contact with an estimated one hundred NVA.

Dabney radioed me at 0301 hours. He was concerned that the NVA were trying to move reinforcements between his position and the FSB perimeter. I told him that we would plaster the area with our 81mm mortars. Minutes later Charlie Company's three 81mm mortars were in action, tearing up the area between the FSB and Delta Company's

NDP. I had to call a check fire when five ACAVs from Delta Troop rolled out of the perimeter to reinforce Dabney's company.

Gunships and TAC air were requested to support the embattled Warrior companies. By 0400 hours, a FAC, call sign Drama Zero Five, was over Delta Company's perimeter along with Moonshine Forty-five, an AC-47 flare ship. Dabney reported one KIA and five men MIA. He also had a number of wounded, but a medevac had to be put on hold until an airstrike was completed. While watching the strike from atop my command bunker, I received a radio message that the southern and western sides of the FSB were taking incoming fire. My 3d Platoon had one man wounded by 12.75mm machine-gun fire. The round shattered the man's knee joint, and his lower leg was hanging by a thread. He was carried under fire to the battalion aid station, where the battalion surgeon struggled to save his life.

Air Force F-100s continued to pound the NVA around Delta Company's positions with napalm, five-hundred-pound bombs, and 20mm cannon fire. Meanwhile, Alpha Company repulsed attackers with fire support provided by a team of Cobra gunships. Reynolds reported that the enemy was breaking contact and fleeing north. The worst of the fighting was over by first light.

The NVA left ninety-two dead in the paddies around Delta and Alpha company positions. Delta Company identified prisoners they took as members of the 271st and 272d NVA regiments, part of an attack force whose objective was Tan Son Nhut Air Base. Their route of march took them right through Dabney's blocking positions. Total losses for the Warrior companies were one man KIA and fifteen WIA, mostly from Delta Company.

FSB Stephanie continued to receive intermittent sniper

fire from the village throughout the morning of 7 May. It wasn't safe outside the bunkers. A headquarters soldier was shot while using a field latrine.

Around noon the sniper fire subsided, and I called my platoon leaders to my CP for a meeting. We were standing outside the bunker when an NVA marksman found the range. An AK-47 round slammed into the side of the CP bunker. Before we could react, we heard a sharp *whack*. First Sergeant Holmes grasped his midsection and doubled over in pain. We pulled up his jungle fatigue shirt. There was no entry wound, just a large purple bruise. Looking at the ground between his feet Holmes bent down and picked up the spent AK-47 round. It was flattened on one side, evidently a ricochet.

Without blinking an eye, Holmes said, "See, I told you officers I was bulletproof."

Mike Hinkley, 2d Platoon leader, calmly said, "Can we finish the briefing inside your bunker, Captain?"

We planned an aggressive defense for the following night. The line platoons would send out night combat patrols to keep the NVA from using the cover of darkness to move in close and give us hell. There was no reason the enemy should own the night, I thought. We tried to pinpoint locations on the map where we thought enemy snipers might deploy.

Around 1600 hours, we received an intelligence report that at least a company of NVA was holed up in the village of Binh Tri Dong just south of the FSB. Their snipers were within easy range of our perimeter. After taking another casualty on the southern perimeter, I went to the battalion commander and proposed a night attack on the village. Mastoris refused, saying that it was "too risky." He had other plans. Bravo Company was south of the village and would attack before dark.

Bravo launched its attack at 1800, but it stalled short of

the village. Lee Smith, the Bravo Company commander, was wounded, as were six enlisted men. Smith refused medical evacuation and stayed with his company. Two other men were killed in the assault. The company had to cross a stretch of open rice paddies to reach the village, and it never got within two hundred meters of the objective.

Shortly after dark, Mike Hinkley reported that his 2d Platoon had spotted some movement about one hundred meters northeast of the FSB perimeter. I instructed him to send out a patrol to check the area. At the same time I ordered Lt. Bob Stanley to send out a patrol to clear the south side of the perimeter between our wire and two paddy dikes that ran parallel to the village. Both patrols returned within the hour without making any enemy contact. I ordered the company to 50-percent alert (half the men sleep while the other half remain on watch) for the rest of the night.

At 0145, 8 May, 2d Platoon reported about twenty NVA soldiers moving through the paddies three hundred meters from the perimeter. Hinkley's M79 grenadiers fired at the enemy patrol, and I called in a fire mission to Mortar Platoon. Lieutenant Hinkley reported that the 81mm mortar and 40mm grenade fire scattered the enemy, and that some had fallen in the barrage. I told him we would check out the area at first light.

At dawn Bravo Company, still holding its positions behind the paddy dikes south of the village, came under RPG fire that killed one man and wounded fourteen others. Three troopers from D/17th Cavalry were also wounded. Ten men were wounded seriously enough to require evacuation. Among the wounded was Capt. Lee Smith, who was hit for the second time in two days. Bravo Company was in bad shape, having lost its company commander, two platoon leaders, and all of its medics except one who was slightly wounded. Capt. Bob Tyson, the Echo Company commander, was flown in to fill in for Smith as temporary commander of Bravo Company.

The enemy still held the village in force despite hammering from artillery and gunships. A number of the houses in this prosperous village had concrete floors, and the NVA were dug in under them. The rubble from the destroyed houses provided excellent cover and concealment for the enemy as they moved from position to position. A frontal assault by a single company was not going to retake the village.

The fight for Binh Tri Dong continued throughout the morning and afternoon. The brigade commander ordered 3/7th Infantry, the Cottonbalers, to take the village. Lieutenant Colonel Ken Hall, the former brigade S-3, had assumed command of the Cottonbalers a few days before. Bravo Company, 4/12th, was attached to Hall's battalion. Taking the village was a formidable task even for Hall's reinforced battalion.

The day was blisteringly hot. Companies of the 3/7th launched their assault from east to west along the northern edge of the village, while Bravo Company struggled to gain a foothold on the south side. Fire control was a problem. The boundary between the Cottonbaler and Warrior battalions ran just north of the village, about three hundred meters from FSB Stephanie's southern perimeter.

Shortly after 1400, the Cottonbalers called a fire mission on some dug-in NVA positions in the village. The 105mm rounds overshot the village and landed in our perimeter. While the artillerymen sorted things out, the 3/7th's attack stalled. By 1500 the Cottonbalers started to withdraw under heavy automatic-weapons and RPG fire. Lieutenant Colonel Hall called for air support.

We had a ringside seat for the airstrike. A pair of F-100s swooped low over the fire base and went into a steep climb after releasing their high-drag five-hundred-pound bombs on enemy positions in the village. A defiant stream of green tracers shot upward from an NVA antiaircraft machine gun, narrowly missing one of the fighters. The earth beneath our feet shook from the bomb detonations, and we felt the shock waves less than a second later. Leaping orange tongues of flame consumed the dwellings. Most of the village was afire. After another bombing run, the jets made several strafing runs, blasting the enemy positions with their cannons. The surviving NVA gunners defiantly fired another stream of green tracers into the air. Clouds of smoke and haze hung over the battered village.

After the airstrike, the enemy continued their sporadic but heavy sniper fire on our perimeter. A gunship team was requested to suppress the fire that we thought was coming from a drainage ditch just south of our perimeter. Bravo Company still was taking heavy fire on the other side of the village, and a medevac was requested to evacuate Bravo's acting commander, Bob Tyson, who sustained a ruptured eardrum. It was a standoff. The village remained under enemy control.

We prepared for night operations as darkness fell. Everyone was tense. We knew from intelligence reports that the NVA still operated in force throughout our area. The 25th Infantry Division, operating to our north, reported contact with a hundred NVA. That enemy force was moving south into our area of operations. The 25th Infantry Division's 3/4th Cavalry pursued them.

I ordered my three rifle platoons to send out LPs at least two hundred meters from the perimeter to provide early warning of any attack on the fire base. Delta Company was still about 1,500 meters to our north-northwest. The NVA had plenty of ground to maneuver between Delta Company and my LPs. Artillery plotted DEFCONs in this no-man's-land, but I was still concerned about this gap.

At 2020 hours, Delta Company opened fire on a group of

NVA attempting to move across the eastern flank of the company position. A sweep of the area yielded five NVA bodies and several weapons. An hour later, Delta Company came under heavy machine-gun fire from the north. Captain Jim Dabney called for his preplanned mortar and artillery fires to suppress the enemy machine-gun fire.

Around midnight Delta Company reported a platoon-size enemy force north of its position. Dabney had deployed his company in a T-shaped ambush and waited for the NVA to close into the kill zone. Delta Company troopers sprang the ambush and killed a number of the enemy. The survivors broke contact and withdrew northward. Gunships were called upon to pursue the fleeing enemy. At 0054 hours, the southern tip of Dabney's T-shaped ambush engaged approximately sixty enemy soldiers who were firing on the company from behind a berm covered with bamboo. Mortar fire drove the enemy from their positions, and they withdrew southwest in the direction of FSB Stephanie.

While I monitored Delta Company's fight on the radio, I ordered my LPs north of the fire base to return to the perimeter. I wanted to be able to deliver unrestricted fire on the northern approaches to our perimeter without risking any casualties from friendly fire.

Delta Company continued to spot enemy soldiers moving on all sides of its ambush location. Mortar and artillery fire were dispersing the enemy formations, but the company continued to receive heavy fire.

I ordered Charlie Company to 100-percent alert, and all along the perimeter the men peered into the darkness with Starlight Scopes. Aerial flares illuminated the area, casting eerie shadows across the landscape.

At 0135 hours, Lieutenant Tuber radioed that 1st Platoon had spotted a group of approximately one hundred NVA moving east to west on the northern side of the perimeter. The NVA troops were strung out in a long single-file formation moving directly toward the no-man's-land between the fire base perimeter and Delta Company's location 1,500 meters to our north.

The 1st Platoon opened fire on the group with machine guns, and I called for mortar fire. We broke up the formation, but smaller groups continued to move westward. My guess was that the enemy was not so much bent on attacking the fire base but was withdrawing west toward the Cambodian border. It appeared they would slip between the fire base and the Delta Company ambush.

I requested permission from Lieutenant Colonel Mastoris to lead a combat patrol to intercept the group. He consented, and I hastily organized the patrol from the men of 1st and 2d platoons. I intended to exit through the wire on the northwestern side of the perimeter, then sweep eastward across the paddies until we made contact. At 0321 hours, some twenty-five of us—two rifle squads, each with an M60 machine gun, and my command group consisting of my two RTOs and my XO, Lt. Carl Frazier—slipped quietly through a gap in the concertina wire. Frazier was getting short and wanted some action. We traveled light, carrying only our weapons, extra bandoliers of ammunition, and two frags per man.

Our patrol moved about two hundred meters to the north of the fire base and began a sweep eastward toward the enemy. We soon ran headlong into the NVA force. We took cover behind a paddy dike and engaged the surprised enemy force with machine-gun and rifle fire. The fire was intense. No more than fifty meters separated us. Machine-gun rounds thudded into the dike in front of us. I ordered one of the squads to provide cover while I low-crawled forward with the other squad to flank the enemy. Green AK-47 tracer rounds zipped through the air inches above our prone bodies. I could see an enemy machine gun firing some twenty meters to my front. Fortunately, the gun was slamming rounds into the dike behind us. I didn't think we had been spotted by the gunners as we were flattened on the ground, but we couldn't assault the enemy until we took out that gun.

I inched forward, slowly angling in on the machine gun. M79 grenadiers from my covering squad were trying to knock out the gun as well. I prayed they had the correct range and wouldn't drop a 40mm round on us. An aerial flare popped to our north and we froze flat on the ground, hoping we wouldn't be spotted. We crawled forward again as the illumination round burned out.

Finally, we were in hand-grenade range. I pulled a frag from my web gear. I saw a muzzle flash from the machine gun; it was about twelve meters to my right front, behind another dike. It was a long throw from the prone position, but I thought I could reach the gun. I lay my CAR15 aside and pulled the pin from the grenade. Gripping the handle tightly, I rose to a kneeling position and heaved the grenade toward the muzzle of the machine gun. I thought the throw was short at first, but the grenade cleared the dike by about two feet. I flattened my body on the ground, burying my face in the mud to await the concussion. Seconds passed, and I thought the grenade could be a dud. As I raised my head slightly, the grenade detonated, blinding me with the flash. A deafening concussion rang in my ears.

The squad jumped to its feet behind me and assaulted the dike, blasting away with M16s. We closed on the NVA and killed fourteen, including the three-man machine-gun crew that had been blown apart by my grenade. We also captured three badly wounded prisoners. The remainder of the enemy, a group of about fifteen, fled north.

I told Frazier to search the bodies, collect the weapons, and guard the wounded NVA while I took one squad to pursue the fleeing enemy. We undertook a running firefight across the dark rice paddies. The NVA were dragging their wounded; whenever they reached a paddy dike, they stopped and fired at us. When we hit the dirt, they took off again toward the next dike.

Then they decided to make a stand behind one of the dikes. We took cover behind a dike facing theirs and returned fire. Without a second squad to provide covering fire, I wasn't going to risk another assault like the last one. I shone my red-filtered flashlight on my map, trying to pinpoint our precise location and the nearest DEFCON plotted on my map. I would adjust the mortar fire from that point. Hoping I had an accurate fix on our location, I called in the fire mission to my mortars.

Jaynes's men manned their tubes. We were close enough to hear the *thunk* of the first 81mm mortar round as it hit the bottom of the mortar tube. Seconds passed as we waited for the round to impact. It detonated about a hundred meters behind and to the right of the enemy's position.

"Left fifty and drop one hundred," I whispered into the handset. The next round dropped about fifteen meters behind the dike. "Fire for effect!" I ordered.

Nine 81mm mortar rounds blew apart the dike to our front. Seconds after the final rounds exploded, we were on our feet moving forward in an assault line. Firing from the hip, we assaulted across the darkened rice paddy. Four NVA bodies, all riddled with shrapnel wounds, lay strewn behind what was left of the dike. I noticed that one of the NVA had a U.S. PRC-25 radio strapped to his back; it was set on frequency 44.00. Later, I was informed that this was one of the frequencies used by Tan Son Nhut Air Base.

We returned to Frazier's location and set up a perimeter defense. The patrol stayed in place until daylight. One of the prisoners died from his wounds shortly before dawn. I thought one of the other two might be an officer, but I wasn't sure. He wasn't wearing any rank insignia, but Frazier had found a Browning 9mm pistol tucked in the man's waistband. NVA enlisted soldiers didn't, as a rule, carry pistols. The man was wounded too seriously to speak, so it was impossible to interrogate him.

At dawn I called for a medevac to take out the wounded prisoners. Both were still breathing as we carried them to the UH-1 and loaded them. I never heard if they survived. Next we gathered the captured enemy weapons and began the trek back to FSB Stephanie. On the way back, we found another dead NVA who had crawled away to a rice paddy. He lay face-down on top of his rifle. The stock of his AK-47 was covered with congealed blood. I grabbed the weapon, a grisly trophy of war, and slung it over my shoulder.

After I briefed Mastoris on our night patrol, I returned to my bunker and fell asleep. First Sergeant Holmes woke me two hours later. He told me that a prisoner reported that an NVA battalion was to attack FSB Stephanie the night before, but Delta and Charlie companies had completely disrupted their plans.

Bravo Company, still south of Binh Tri Dong, also captured a prisoner who stated that U.S. airstrikes and artillery had destroyed most of the three companies that held the village. One unit had tried to break out early that same morning, but was unsuccessful. The prisoner further stated that most of the survivors were wounded too badly to surrender. It was impossible to tell if the prisoner was telling the truth, and I wasn't buying his story. If the enemy were going to try a breakout, it would be during darkness. Besides, we were still taking sniper fire from the village.

Captain Lee Smith, whose wounds had been patched up, returned to his company later that morning. His back had been riddled with tiny shards of B-40 rocket shrapnel, but none of the shards was large enough to do any serious damage. He was determined to see the fight to its conclusion.

Delta Company spent the day sweeping the areas of the previous night's contacts; it located more enemy KIA and their weapons. They also found a Chinese-made radio and field telephone. Most of the enemy dead were from the 246th NVA Battalion.

Attacks on the village of Binh Tri Dong by three rifle companies of the 3/7th Infantry and Bravo Company, 4/12th, continued throughout the morning and afternoon of 9 May. The backbone of the enemy resistance was broken after numerous ground assaults, artillery barrages, and eighteen sorties of TAC air. The final assault on the village by the 3/7th Cottonbalers met only scattered resistance. After a sweep of the village, the Cottonbalers reported finding a total of thirty-six enemy bodies. Many others were blown to bits or buried in the rubble. The village was in bad shape; fifty-four structures were completely destroyed, and another twenty-seven were damaged.

At 1700 Bravo Company was released from control of the 3/7th Infantry and ordered back to FSB Stephanie. The battle for Binh Tri Dong was over.

The area north of Stephanie was still contested by the enemy. Before dark several ACAVs departed the base perimeter to resupply Delta Company with ammunition and .50-caliber machine-gun replacement parts. Due to its vulnerable location, the infantry company was issued a .50-caliber heavy machine gun, a weapon rarely found in a light infantry company.

Intelligence reports indicated that more NVA units were in our AO. Based on this information, I again put Charlie Company on full alert all along the base perimeter. We caught a few hours of sleep during daylight hours and stayed awake throughout the hours of darkness. A full-scale ground attack on the fire base was still a possibility. Darkness soon enveloped the fire base, and Charlie Company troopers began slipping through the rolls of concertina wire surrounding the base to occupy four LPs. In view of the previous night's firefights, this was not a popular assignment among the infantrymen.

Checking my short-timer calendar, I noted that it was Thursday, 9 May. My scheduled departure for a five-day R&R to Bangkok was only two days away. I wondered if I would get to go. I needed a break, but my own well-being was not my primary concern.

All remained quiet until 2020, when Delta Company began experiencing small enemy probes of their night positions. Within the hour, Delta was in contact with an estimated battalion of NVA. Once again, the Warriors of Delta Company fought off the NVA elements. As Spooky illuminated the battlefield with magnesium flares, helicopter gunships decimated the attackers, followed by three separate strikes by high-performance aircraft. On one of the strikes, napalm canisters landed perilously close to several Delta positions, but no serious friendly casualties resulted. It was all over by midnight. Delta Company called a dust-off for its wounded and swept the area around its perimeter, finding twenty-four enemy dead in the process. The heaviest fighting of the May Offensive was over for the Warrior battalion. Delta Company was awarded the Presidential Unit Citation for its role in the battle.

Dawn broke quietly over FSB Stephanie. It was Friday, 10 May. Smoke still rose from the ruins of Binh Tri Dong. ACAVs from D Troop, 17th Cavalry, rumbled northward on a resupply mission to Delta Company.

I visited the battalion TOC, where I learned that the 199th Infantry Brigade had a new commander, Brig. Gen. Franklin M. Davis. He replaced our interim commander, Col. Fred Davison, who assumed command after the departure of General Forbes. Forbes had given me command of Charlie Company in January, and I had a high respect for him. Davison was a soldier's soldier who always went the extra mile for his troops, so we were all pleased that he would remain with the brigade as deputy commander.

The skies opened up in a torrential downpour later that afternoon. The rainy season was upon us. As twilight approached and the rain tapered off to a fine drizzle, I stood staring at a bulldozer working along the perimeter. The operator was scraping the mud to form a dirt berm between the bunkers. I wondered if the dirt berm would be washed away by the daily monsoon rains. I was relieved that the heavy fighting was over, but at the same time I felt despondent. The death and destruction that surrounded us troubled my soul. The brutality and savagery of this war had changed my life and the lives of the young soldiers in my charge forever. We were no longer innocents. I could see no end to this war.

chapter thirteen

an opportunity missed

> O that I had wings like a dove: for then would I flee
> away, and be at rest.
>
> —Psalms 55:14

On the morning of 12 May, I packed my gear and caught a helicopter ride back to Long Binh. The fighting around FSB Stephanie had slacked off, and I was confident that my XO could handle the perimeter-defense mission for the next five days.

I had planned to spend Saturday night at Camp Frenzell-Jones, then depart the following day for Camp Alpha in Saigon, the processing center for troops going on R&R. My flight to Bangkok was scheduled for Sunday afternoon.

After checking in at my orderly room and signing a few papers, I visited the PX and bought some civilian clothes for my trip. I ate a hot meal at the battalion mess hall, showered, donned a clean uniform, and headed for the officers club, where I took a seat at the bar.

Staff officers drifted into the bar in their starched jungle fatigues and spit-shined boots. As I nursed my beer, a Filipino rock band started playing their first set of the night. A few minutes later the bartender informed me that I had a phone call, then directed me to a small office where I could take it. It was Maj. Ed Kelley, the Warrior battalion XO.

"Bob, I just wanted to let you know that we airmobiled your company out on an operation this afternoon. They made contact with an NVA unit and took several casualties.

The company has dug in for the night, and as far as we know everything is under control. They'll be extracted tomorrow."

Damn it! I thought, trying to compose myself.

"Any friendly KIAs?" I asked.

"There was one man who was badly wounded, but he was still alive when he was dusted off."

"Are they still in contact?"

"Not at the moment. I just wanted to let you know that things didn't go well. Lieutenant Stanley led the assault, and the company's digging in for the night."

"Do you need me back out there?"

"That's not my call. I just wanted to let you know."

I made up my mind immediately. I returned to my company area, grabbed my field gear and CAR15 from the supply room, and headed for the brigade's "Fireball" aviation section.

The brigade aviation section kept one UH-1 on standby at the base camp. I located the pilot and managed to convince him to radio the brigade forward TOC to get permission to fly me out to my company's position. Lieutenant Colonel Don Bolduc, the brigade S-3, came up on the radio and asked me gruffly, "What in the hell do you want one of my C&C ships for, Captain? Does Warrior Six know what you're doing?"

Choosing my words carefully, I replied, "I spoke to Warrior Five, and I think they need me on the ground."

"Okay, so long as your boss knows about it," Bolduc grumbled.

I climbed aboard the slick and we flew south into the night. The UH-1 touched down in a rice paddy next to a narrow dirt road, and I jumped out. As the ship lifted off, Bob Stanley led me forward to where my platoons were dug in perpendicular to the road. About 250 meters ahead, the road ended at a canal. At this point, a narrow footbridge crossed the canal. A small village sat on the opposite side.

I asked Stanley to bring me up to date on what had happened earlier in the day. He said that Charlie Company had landed on an LZ about five hundred meters to the south and then swept north toward the canal. There was no sign of the enemy, so he told his men to cross the canal using the narrow footbridge. When the lead squad began to cross the bridge in single file, the enemy opened up from the village with machine-gun and RPG fire. The point squad had three men wounded, but it managed to withdraw with them. Specialist Dave Loughrie, 3d Platoon medic, was credited with saving the lives of two men, Specialist Stokes and Private First Class Grammar. Loughrie moved forward under heavy fire to administer first aid and then carried the men to safety. He was assisted by Privates First Class Vito Graziano and Dale Bourland, two of the riflemen from 3d Platoon. Unfortunately, no one thought to recover the wounded soldiers' weapons. After pulling back about 250 meters, the two platoons formed a defensive perimeter and called in a dust-off for the wounded.

I asked Stanley if the enemy was still located in the village. He didn't know. I had him show me how he had his men deployed. The men seemed despondent and indifferent.

Lieutenant Stanley was my most-seasoned rifle platoon leader, but he had never before led the company on an operation. From what I heard, it seemed that Charlie Company had been bested in the fight, and this made me mad as hell. Stanley bore the brunt of my anger.

"Lieutenant, the first thing we're going to do is recover those weapons you lost," I said angrily.

"We can't, Sir. The VC have the area covered with machine guns."

"Wrong answer! We'll suppress them with artillery fire," I responded.

"The arty wouldn't give me a fire mission earlier. They said there could be civilians in the village."

"I'll handle that. You get some of your men together and go get those fucking weapons now!" I said.

I radioed FSB Stephanie for artillery fire. The fire direction officer disapproved the fire mission.

"Those coordinates are in a village," the artillery fire direction officer said.

"I'll take responsibility for that," I responded.

I suspected that if there were any civilians remaining in the village, they would be hiding in bunkers and tunnels dug deep beneath their village.

"All right, I'll fire the mission, but it's your ass that's on the line," he replied.

While the howitzer rounds slammed into the village, Stanley led his men forward to recover the lost weapons. They took no fire. After recovering the weapons, we planned a dawn attack on the village. We wouldn't try to cross the foot bridge. Instead, we would ford the canal at two locations: one upstream from the village, the other downstream. The reserve platoon would set up on the south bank near the bridge and provide suppressive fire during the crossings.

We began the crossings in the morning mist that hung low over the canal. The M60 machine gunners opened up on the hooches across the canal. Red tracers tore through the thatched huts and started a few fires. The two canal crossings were unopposed, and the flanking platoons entered the village from opposite ends.

The village was deserted. The only signs of the enemy were empty AK-47 and .51-caliber shell casings. I radioed the TOC and requested an airmobile extraction to FSB Stephanie. No air assets were available, but I was promised that tracks from D Troop, 17th Cavalry, would be dispatched to transport us. We waited until early afternoon for the tracks to arrive. When they did, my weary troops climbed aboard for the ride back to Stephanie.

As we rode back, I thought about how disappointed I

was with Charlie Company's performance, and more so my own. At that moment I realized that I had failed to prepare my lieutenants to take over the company in my absence. This was a huge mistake, because I could become a casualty like anyone else. I had let my lieutenants down, and more important, had put the soldiers of Charlie Company at risk.

Lieutenant Colonel Mastoris was airborne directing an airmobile assault, so I returned gloomily to my bunker. I had missed my R&R flight and felt lousy about myself. Outgoing artillery fire shook the bunker walls and ceiling as I fell into a deep sleep.

chapter fourteen

war so terrible

I've seen fire, and I've seen rain.
—JAMES TAYLOR,
"Fire and Rain"

The Paris peace negotiations began on 13 May, then stalled. The U.S. and North Vietnamese couldn't agree on the shape of the conference table. Meanwhile, the war continued unabated. Daily downpours flooded the rice paddies around FSB Stephanie. The dirt berm between the perimeter bunkers was slowly washing away. Grunts removed layers of sandbags from the tops of their leaky bunkers and laid clear sheets of plastic before replacing them. The bottoms of the bunkers were flooding, so the troops used wooden ammo boxes as flooring. These attempts to waterproof the bunkers met with little success, but they kept the men busy.

One morning I plodded through the black, sucking mud that covered the road leading to Binh Tri Dong. Beside the road lay the bloated carcasses of two water buffalo killed by artillery fire. Their legs were outstretched in unlifelike poses. As I entered the village, I surveyed the damage. Most of the houses were now nothing more than piles of rubble, but a few remained standing, only pockmarked by shrapnel and bullets. The villagers had returned and were poking through the rubble while a group of young boys played nearby. The boys ran toward me, asking for C rations. I dug into the deep side pockets of my jungle fatigue trousers and

171

retrieved two chocolate bars. I was deeply saddened. We
had destroyed what we'd come to save.

The Warriors of Charlie Company were displaying more
and more of a fire base mentality. Drinking and pot smoking among the battalion support troops, artillerymen, and
some of my own men was no secret. The battalion beer and
soda tent was open from morning to night. Rumor had it
that the profits from sales were running about $12,000 a
month. Vietnamese civilians who returned to the village
were trading sex and drugs for MPC (U.S. Military Payment Certificates used in lieu of greenbacks in Vietnam)
and materials to rebuild their homes. I suspected that a PF
platoon was involved in the drug dealing. Troops from
Stephanie sneaked off to the village whenever they saw the
opportunity. The daily torrential rains did nothing to improve morale. The longer we stayed at Stephanie, the more
the Warriors lost their edge.

The NVA had retreated to their Cambodian sanctuaries,
but local Vietcong guerrillas continued to operate in our
area. Charlie Company conducted daylight and night patrols around FSB Stephanie, trying to make contact with
these enemy units.

Local VC were reported to be infiltrating Binh Tri Dong
at night, so I decided to send a night ambush patrol into the
village. The 2d Platoon drew the honors. Mike Hinkley led
the patrol as it slipped silently through the wire, crossed the
paddies, and entered the village. The lieutenant had an
eerie feeling that his patrol was being watched, but he kept
moving toward his ambush site. The following day he dis-
covered that he and his men had walked right through a recon platoon ambush. The outnumbered recon platoon
grunts mistook Hinkley's platoon for NVA and had been
too scared to react.

In addition to the local patrols around Stephanie, Charlie

Company was on call for airmobile operations. The southwestern approaches to Saigon were a major security concern for MACV, so a series of daily airmobile operations was planned along the numerous canals and waterways leading toward the city. Another area of concern, to the west of Stephanie, was a large pineapple plantation that served as a base and staging area for NVA units on their way to Saigon.

Because most of the intelligence reports were a day late and a dollar short, the airmobile operations met with little success. We landed in the flooded paddies and pineapple fields and conducted strenuous sweeps through the muddy terrain. Booby traps were a constant hazard. We avoided walking on the paddy dikes, which were often booby trapped or mined. Instead, we struggled through the sucking mud of the paddies. The banks of the streams were especially treacherous. Each step through the soft muck was torture, and every few steps a man would sink in mud up to his crotch. The gnarled roots of the mangroves could twist an ankle or a knee in a second. The putrid stench of rotting vegetation permeated the stifling humid air, and canteens were emptied quickly. After each stream crossing, the men checked their bodies for leeches. It was not unusual to find one or more of the three-inch-long slimy, black-brown creatures affixed to a shin or calf, feasting on blood. Nests of ants were another hazard in the nipa palm swamps. A man might suffer a hundred ant bites in a matter of seconds if he stumbled into a nest.

These operations were sheer hell, and the sun was usually well into its western quadrant before we received orders for an airmobile extraction back to the fire base. I alternated platoons on these operations but accompanied each one with my command group. As a result, the members of the command group were wearing down fast. My senior RTO, Bob Archibald, had lost about twenty pounds, and when I heard the S-2 needed an enlisted man for the TOC, I had him reassigned. He had more than earned it.

On 21 May, the 199th Brigade left the area southwest of Saigon and moved north of Long Binh. Unfortunately, the Warrior battalion was left behind under the operational control of the 25th Infantry Division. We continued operations in the same miserable terrain that we had been working in throughout the month of May. The frequency of airmobile operations increased to almost a daily basis for the rifle companies of the Warrior battalion. Charlie Company continued as the fire-base security company, but we were on daily standby for such operations. The men were sullen and my own depression deepened as the month of May drew to a close.

chapter fifteen

melting point

Abiit, excessit, evasit.
(He departed, he withdrew, he strode off.)
—Cicero

June 1968

On 2 June, I awoke before dawn and listened as the platoons radioed in their SITREPs. It had rained only once during the night, but it was a very hard rain and my jungle fatigues were soaked. I rummaged through an open case of C rations in search of a can of fruit and grunted a "good morning" to Allen Pollastrini, who had the morning radio watch.

There were red and blue hues in the dawn that morning. Anticipating an uneventful day, I checked my platoon positions on the fire base perimeter and stopped by the battalion TOC. Staff officers and NCOs were gathered around the map boards. I picked up pieces of information as I eavesdropped on conversations and radio transmissions. Major Gillespie, the S-3, informed me that Delta Company would conduct an airmobile assault later that morning. I was surprised, because the Delta CO, Jim Dabney, was on R&R. His XO, Lt. Wayne Smith, would lead the assault. Gillespie reminded me that Charlie Company was on call to reinforce Delta Company if needed. I studied the operations map and copied the grid coordinates of Delta Company's LZ on my own map.

I then returned to my CP and called my platoon leaders to brief them on Delta Company's airmobile operation. I told them that if our company was committed, 1st and 3d platoons would deploy along with my command group.

Anticipating the long day ahead, I sat down to read a copy of *Stars and Stripes*. The presidential campaign was heating up back in the States, and it looked like Bobby Kennedy was going to overtake Hubert Humphrey as the Democratic frontrunner. I was following the primary campaigns with interest. The paper also published casualty lists. I read that May 1968 had been the most costly month of the war to date, even exceeding the Tet Offensive months of January and February. I wondered if June would be any better.

Delta Company's airmobile did not begin until mid-afternoon. I spotted the helicopters descending in a long line toward Delta Company's pick-up zone. Moments later the fully loaded Hueys emerged over the horizon, flying toward an LZ ten kilometers to the south. The howitzers on the other end of the fire base began belching smoke and flame as the LZ prep began. Fifteen minutes later Delta Company's first lift was on the ground reporting a cold LZ. Chances that Charlie Company would not be needed now improved.

My hopes shattered thirty minutes later when Delta Company reported contact. One of Delta's platoons was in a hot firefight in a bunker complex along a canal. They had a KIA and a couple of wounded. Lieutenant Smith, acting CO, had landed with another platoon on a second LZ a kilometer downstream and was moving toward the fighting. Seconds later I received a call from Lieutenant Colonel Mastoris, who was airborne in his C&C ship. He was on his way to pick me up; he wanted me to get a look at the area in the event Delta Company had to be reinforced.

I grabbed my web gear, map, and a PRC-25 radio and ran to the helipad. The howitzers continued to fire in support of Delta Company. I knew that the artillery wouldn't be much help if the VC were fighting from bunkers. Most VC bunkers could survive a direct hit from a 105mm howitzer.

Mastoris's C&C bird hovered a foot off the PSP landing pad. I sprinted through the whirlwind of sand and grit blown up by rotor wash and climbed on board. The battalion commander, his artillery liaison officer, S-3 Air, and radio operators took up all the seats inside the Huey, so I sat on the floor.

I grabbed a headset from the C&C console so I could talk to the CO. He said that he had requested an airstrike on the bunker complex, and that Delta Company's platoons were pulling back to a safe standoff distance.

The pilot flew south, avoiding the gun-target line of the howitzers. Five minutes later we were orbiting overhead the bunker complex. A team of Cobra gunships was at work, firing rockets into a thick growth of nipa palm next to a stream, while an Air Force FAC orbited a thousand feet above us in an OV-10. I assumed the VC bunkers were hidden in the foliage.

Yellow smoke billowed skyward from behind a paddy dike about a hundred meters from the stream. Infantrymen were sprawled behind the dike. This was Delta Company's forward position. The gunships had suppressed the enemy fire with their rockets and miniguns. Suddenly, the Cobras broke off and flew north along the stream.

Taking up where the Cobras left off, the FAC placed his OV-10 into a steep dive and fired two white phosphorous rockets at the enemy bunkers. Seconds later, the C&C ship banked sharply to the right. I saw an F-100 fighter scream past the Huey on its attack run. The jet wash of the fighter shook the helicopter, and our pilot fought for control. The door gunners were leaning forward over their machine guns trying to follow the path of the jet. Shaken, the pilot of the C&C ship flew toward a safer orbit away from the strike area.

Once the airstrike was completed, Mastoris ordered the C&C ship to fly up the stream another kilometer to an area where the Cobras had spotted more bunkers. When we were over the suspected enemy bunkers, the Warrior CO came up on the intercom and said he wanted to select an LZ nearby to insert Charlie Company. We picked an LZ out of range of the bunkers, which were concealed in a small patch of ground next to a canal. Banana trees and other foliage provided natural camouflage for the enemy fortifications. Mastoris wanted Charlie Company to find out if the enemy occupied these positions. After another pass over the area, Mastoris ordered the pilot to return to Stephanie so I could prepare for the airmobile insertion.

By the time I landed at Stephanie, 1st and 3d platoons were already moving out of the fire base and lining up by chalk loads alongside the slippery paddy dikes north of the perimeter. The daily rains had turned the paddies into miniature lakes, and walking through them with a forty-pound rucksack was an extremely fatiguing exercise. It was around 1600 hours.

After I briefed my lieutenants at the CP, I followed them through a gap in the concertina wire to the pick-up zone. I felt uneasy about this operation. We had never been in the area before, and we only had a few hours of daylight remaining.

The late afternoon sun was hot and shimmering off the bright green rice paddies. It eased the pain in our sore muscles and stiff joints. Thick gray clouds began to form on the horizon, foreshadowing a late afternoon downpour. My RTO, Allen Pollastrini, handed me the handset to take a call from the battalion commander. Mastoris said that the helicopters were inbound.

Ten UH-1s in tight trail formation touched down in the paddies. We ran to board the slicks as their rotor wash sprayed brown muddy water over our sweat-drenched jungle fatigues. The chopper pilots brought their engines to full RPM, which created a pulsating roar as we climbed aboard.

As we lifted off, I experienced a brief moment of exhilaration followed by a dark premonition of what awaited us.

The slicks flew southwest in staggered trail formation over a patchwork of rice paddies and canals. The five riflemen on board sat cross-legged on the floor with their M16s propped upright between their knees. As the choppers began their descent, they slid toward the doors.

Peering at the landscape below, I saw artillery rounds exploding in the nipa palm growth along a canal. Cobra gunships were blasting a palm grove with rockets. As the Hueys settled toward the paddies, the door gunners fired bursts into the paddy dikes. The pilots flared the noses of their ships upward as they settled toward the ground.

We leaped into the muddy rice paddy and ran toward the cover of a nearby dike. The CP group moved forward with 2d Platoon toward the nipa palm growth bordering the canal. The 1st Platoon advanced toward the palm grove. I radioed to battalion that the LZ was cold. I glanced at my watch and noted that it was a few minutes past 1700.

Automatic-weapons fire suddenly erupted from a camouflaged bunker in the palm grove. I could see rounds splattering into the paddy mud in front of the advancing infantrymen. The grunts returned fire. Tuber's lead squad charged toward the enemy bunker but was caught in a crossfire from a second bunker. Specialist Fourth Grade Lloyd Starkey, a husky twenty-four-year-old from Hardy, Virginia, was killed instantly. A second burst killed twenty-one-year-old Pfc. Cliff Bailey from Eureka, Kansas. Bailey was a relative newcomer to the company, but his easygoing Midwestern manner had earned him many friends in his platoon. Two other men were wounded, but not seriously. One was Sgt. Jerold Partch, who earned his third Purple Heart in six months.

As 1st Platoon withdrew with their casualties, I radioed for gunship support. I couldn't see the targets from my position, so I told my RTOs to follow me toward 1st Platoon's forward location. The 2d Platoon provided covering fire as we moved across the rice paddy. AK-47 rounds kicked up bits of paddy mud as we ran forward. I returned fire with a couple of unaimed bursts from my CAR15.

After we reached 1st Platoon's position, I took a long drink from my canteen, almost choking on the tepid water. Peering over the paddy dike, I could see Tuber's point squad withdrawing toward our position. The men were half-carrying, half-dragging their dead and wounded. The edge of the palm grove was less than fifty meters away from the paddy dike, but it seemed the struggling men would never reach us. The remainder of 1st and 2nd platoons were providing covering fire, but the *crack* and *pop* of AK rounds continued over our heads.

I laid my CAR15 on top of the dike and rushed forward to the squad in the middle of the paddy. I grabbed the heels of Bailey's jungle boots and lifted them out of the paddy mud while another man hoisted his upper body. It took us a couple more minutes to carry the bodies back to the dike. There was still some enemy fire coming at us, but it was ragged and badly aimed.

Tuber directed the Cobra gunship team into the bunker area with deadly effect. Mastoris directed artillery fire from his C&C ship into the nipa palm growth across the canal. By the time we reached the cover of the paddy dike, Mastoris was on the radio asking for a SITREP.

I grabbed the handset to answer his call: "Warrior Six, this is Marauder Six. Over."

"Marauder Six, this is Warrior Six. You're breaking up and unreadable. Over."

"Goddamn handset is wet!" I barked at Pollastrini. "I thought I told you to wrap it in a plastic battery cover!"

"I've brought a spare handset, Captain. Just let me get it out of my ruck."

When I finally made radio contact with Mastoris, he told me that the 25th Division CG was inbound to our area. The division commander wanted to evacuate our dead and wounded on his C&C ship. There was no way I was going to risk bringing in a two-star's C&C ship into a hot LZ to evacuate two KIAs. The wounded were in no immediate danger. We would have had to secure the area first and knock out those bunkers. Mastoris agreed and flew off to check on Delta Company's fight down the canal.

A few minutes later we saw the 25th Division CG's Huey, with its Tropic Lightning insignia on the nose, as it bore down on our location.

The squelch on my radio broke. "Marauder Six, this is Lightning Six. Mark your location with smoke. I'm inbound to evacuate your casualties. Over."

Damn it, I thought, go get your Distinguished Flying Cross on someone else's LZ. I grabbed the handset, hoping Mastoris would back me up on this one.

"This is Marauder Six. We have incoming fire from fifty meters away and can't mark an LZ. Over."

"Marauder Six. I say again bring me in so I can dust off your casualties. Over."

"This is Marauder Six. I'll have to move them back a couple hundred meters. Over."

"This is Lightning Six. I don't have fuel to stay on station that long. Over."

"This is Marauder Six. Roger that. There's no serious wounded. Recommend you refuel. Over."

"This is Lightning Six. I'm leaving your area. Out!"

The gunships continued their strikes on the palm grove and finally knocked out the two enemy bunkers. I radioed for a dust-off for our KIAs and WIAs.

The gunships had done their work well. Both enemy bunkers had taken multiple rocket hits. We pulled two NVA bodies from one bunker and a third body from the other. A fourth enemy body lay spread-eagled in the mud. Taking no chances, a squad leader in 1st Platoon pumped a burst of M16 rounds into the inert form lying in the mud.

My radio crackled to life. A FAC was putting in an air-strike across the canal. More enemy bunkers had been spotted in this area by the gunships. I looked skyward just in time to see a jet fighter release a high-drag five-hundred-pound bomb. It seemed to be coming right at us. Several men dove into a drainage ditch. I almost did the same, but the falling bomb sailed over the palm grove and into the paddies on the opposite side of the canal. The earth shook violently under our feet. It began to rain.

We set up a perimeter around the edge of the palm grove in the hope of being extracted before dark. There didn't appear to be any reason to stay in the area. We had done our job.

About 1800 hours, the battalion TOC radioed that there were no lift assets available; Charlie Company would have to remain in the area overnight. Delta Company would remain in position about a kilometer and a half down the canal, having finally overrun the other bunker complex. The grunts were none too pleased as they dug muddy foxholes and set out trip flares and Claymores.

Lightning danced wickedly in the twilight sky. Everyone's mood was somber. We had lost two good men and two more wounded in a miserable little fight against an enemy squad.

The rain subsided as darkness fell, and our main concern became the swarms of mosquitoes that attacked us from our wet surroundings. The men ignored the foulness of the muddy water as it slowly filled the holes they had dug. They were too tired to notice.

I ordered a 50-percent alert for the night and dozed fitfully. The almost simultaneous muffled explosions of two grenades jarred me back into consciousness.

"What the hell's going on?"

"It's 2d Platoon," Pollastrini responded. "Someone thought

they heard movement in the canal, like someone swimming, so they threw a couple of frags in the water."

I dozed off again a minute later.

A few minutes after midnight, Pollastrini shook my shoulder.

"Wake up, Captain. First Platoon's reporting movement to their front."

I strained my eyes, but it was too dark to spot anything more than a few yards away. Nevertheless, we could hear water splashing the paddy. It sounded like at least a company of NVA out there, moving right toward us.

I radioed my two platoon leaders and told them to open fire when I fired a hand-held aerial flare. We could see the dark shapes moving toward us as I slapped the cap of the flare against the palm of my hand to set off the detonator. The flare rocketed skyward and burst. The riflemen, machine gunners, and grenadiers opened fire immediately. Under the flare light, we could make out a herd of about twenty water buffalo stampeding back across the paddy. We were relieved, but no one was laughing.

My jungle fatigues were damp from rain and perspiration. I began to shiver and wrapped my poncho tight around my body, wondering if I had malaria. Realizing I wouldn't sleep again, I waited for the dawn.

We crossed the canal the next morning and searched more bunkers, where we found medical supplies and a stash of rice. I radioed FSB Stephanie and requested an airmobile extraction. The two-day operation was a costly one for Charlie Company. We had lost two more good men.

Two days later we learned that Robert Kennedy had been gunned down in California after a triumphant presidential primary win in that state. He was regarded by many as the only candidate who could end the war in Vietnam and resolve the racial violence that was tearing the country apart. I grieved for him along with Starkey and Bailey.

*   *   *

The final three weeks of my command in Charlie Company remain a murky blur in my memory. According to First Sergeant Holmes, Charlie Company was finally relieved of its fire base security mission at Stephanie during the second week of June. We moved to a position forever referred to by members of Charlie Company as "the mud hole." I recall nothing of the move, or the new location. I do remember that I slept briefly and fitfully and always awoke in an irritable state. More than five months of accumulated stress welled up inside my psyche, ready to burst. My thoughts were disordered and I had difficulty focusing on even the most routine tasks. For the first time in my life, I began to suffer from almost constant migraine headaches. My platoon leaders and first sergeant all knew that I was wound too tight, but they said nothing.

During mid-June, Charlie Company made a series of airmobile assaults into the pineapple plantation. We sustained more casualties, mostly from booby traps. I have no recollection of the details of these operations. My recall is limited to sensory images: the dizzying smell of JP4 aviation fuel, sand kicked up by the rotor blades stinging my face, the *whack whack* sound of rotor blades above my head, the sickening dull *thump* of an exploding booby trap, and the cries of the wounded.

Charlie Company returned to FSB Stephanie on 18 June. I hated the fire base with its smell of burning human waste and rat-infested bunkers reeking with mildew and sweat. The mid-June heat was oppressive, bringing on more migraines. Each afternoon the rains came in torrential downpours. Suffering from insomnia, I took to wandering around the perimeter at night. I convinced myself that Stephanie was going to be hit by a VC sapper attack. There was legitimate reason for my concern. A few weeks before, C Company, 2/3d Infantry, had been attacked in their NDP by a VC sapper unit during a driving rainstorm. Captain Vesa Alakulppi and seven of his men were killed in the attack.

A tragic event on 24 June further depressed me. Lieutenant Colonel Ken Hall, commander of the 3/7th Infantry, was killed when his C&C ship crashed after takeoff from a refueling pad at Nha Be. Three members of Hall's battle staff also died when the helicopter crashed into the river. I had worked for Hall when I first arrived in-country and I had the highest admiration for him.

On a cloudy night during the last week of June, I awoke from a disturbed sleep, convinced that VC sappers had penetrated the perimeter. In a dreamlike state, I ran from the bunker and into the darkness. I stumbled and fell into the concertina wire in front of the bunker. I thought I saw shadowy figures darting between the bunkers moving toward me. I buried my face in the mud, expecting a round in the back of my head. I don't know how long I remained on the muddy ground. First Sergeant Holmes found me before dawn when he began his check of the perimeter. He led me back to the command bunker. I was babbling incoherently about a sapper attack.

I am still unable to comprehend what happened to me that night. Perhaps I experienced a delayed reaction to some earlier combat experience. Months of accumulated stress had finally overtaken me.

The following morning Charlie Company was again ordered to conduct an airmobile assault. Over Holmes's objections, I led the two-platoon assault. We trekked through the paddies and mangrove swamps in the stifling heat, finding no trace of an enemy. Late that afternoon we were extracted.

Holmes was waiting for me at the CP. He wanted to talk. He said a rumor had spread through the company that I had totally lost it. Then he recounted my deteriorating mental state over the past weeks. I agreed to go talk with the battalion commander.

I found Lieutenant Colonel Mastoris in his bunker and asked permission to speak with him. Filled with emotion, I poured out my innermost thoughts and feelings to him. I'm sure that he knew that I was close to the edge as he listened compassionately. Then he told me that he had planned to re-assign me as battalion S-3 Air in a few days, but would now send me on R&R the following day. Captain Bob Woodard, battalion S-4, would assume command of Charlie Company. I asked Mastoris if I could be assigned as an advisor to the Vietnamese rather than stay in the battalion. I didn't want to see another American soldier killed or wounded during my tour. He refused, saying that my experience was needed on the battalion staff. I saluted the colonel and walked back to my bunker. At that moment, I felt a sense of guilt leaving Charlie Company. Combat command is a terrible burden, but the highest of privileges for an infantry officer. I had been in Vietnam for nine months, and in command of Charlie Company for six. I was mentally and physically worn out.

Two days later I caught an R&R flight to Bangkok. Arriv-ing at Bangkok's crowded Don Muang Airport, I claimed my bags and hailed a taxi, opting out of the briefings at the R&R center. The Thai taxi driver tried to direct me to a GI R&R hotel, where he ensured me that I would meet some beautiful Thai girls. He was surprised when I replied in Thai with di-rections to the University Hotel located off Rama IV Road near Chulalongkon University. It was a quiet, medium-priced place with a decent restaurant where I had usually stayed when stationed in Thailand. Few Americans ever stayed at the hotel, and it was several miles from the R&R red-light district. I wanted to decompress in a quieter setting.

After checking into my room, I filled the bathtub with steaming hot water. I had tried to scrub myself clean in the shower before leaving Long Binh, but as I sat in the steaming tub I saw the clear hot water suddenly change to a muddy reddish brown color. I tried to scrub the layers of grime from my arms and legs. The scrubbing opened some of the sores and bamboo scratches on my forearms. Cuts never completely healed in the hot, humid climate of Vietnam. I also had a painful white-phosphorus burn on my right forearm. I stared in the mirror while I shaved. The peeling sunburned face that stared back at me was barely recognizable. It had aged several years in the past nine months. There were wrinkles and dark circles around my eyes from squinting in the bright tropical sunlight and a lack of sleep.

I laid down on the cool, freshly laundered sheets and experienced a welcome sense of relief. The stress and tension of the past weeks began to melt away. It was as if I had just awakened from a hellish nightmare and was now trying to go back to quiet sleep. I wanted to fall asleep and not wake up until this senseless war was over.

I slept for fourteen hours, awakening in midafternoon. After ordering a steak and french fries in the hotel restaurant, I telephoned a girl that I had met the previous summer. Her mother was Thai, and her father was Dutch. She was the most beautiful Eurasian woman I had ever seen. We had dated several times when I was in the city during the summer of 1967. Her parents were not pleased to have their only daughter in a relationship with an American soldier, but they accepted me over time. Mostly, we ate at the city's best Thai restaurants and went to American movies that were very popular with the Thais. I was crestfallen when her mother told me she was attending nursing school in Amsterdam.

Disappointed, I headed for a Special Forces hangout, the Three Sisters Bar, where I tried to drown my sorrows in Singha beer. I did the tourist scene for the next four days. I visited the floating markets and cruised down the Chaophraya River past glistening white Buddhist temples with domes covered in gold leaf. I shopped for gifts for family members at the jewelry stores, and each night I dined at one of my favorite restaurants. Then I visited the nightclubs before returning to my hotel. The five days passed all too quickly, and I soon found myself on a flight headed back to Saigon.

I rejoined the Warrior battalion at FSB Stephanie. As S-3 Air, I was responsible for planning and coordinating air-mobile and air support for the Warrior battalion's operations. My days were spent working in the TOC and flying command-and-control missions with the battalion commander and S-3. Charlie Company was finally relieved of the fire base security mission and departed Stephanie.

On 1 September 1968, newly promoted Brig. Gen. Frederic E. Davison took command of the 199th Light Infantry Brigade after Brig. Gen. Franklin Davis was wounded in action. The Redcatcher Brigade continued in good hands.

On 20 September 1968, Gen. Creighton Abrams, commander of U.S. forces in Vietnam, awarded me the Distinguished Service Cross in a ceremony at FSB Stephanie. The award was for my actions as commander of Charlie Company during the January Tet Offensive. An honor guard from Charlie Company led by 1st Sgt. George Holmes participated in the ceremony. That meant more to me than the medal.

My tour with the Warriors of the 4th Battalion, 12th Infantry, ended on 11 October 1968, when I rotated back to the States. Three weeks later, President Johnson announced the complete cessation of air, naval, and artillery bombardment north of the 20th parallel and agreed to admit the National Liberation Front to the Paris peace talks, breaking a long stalemate in the negotiations. Our country was desperately seeking a way out of Vietnam.

epilogue

Thy firmness makes my circle just,
And makes me end, where I begun.
—JOHN DONNE,
"A Valediction:
Forbidding Mourning"

It was early evening on 25 August 1971. As I stood next to my Vietnamese counterpart in knee-high grass, I looked around the LZ where ARVN airborne soldiers clad in camouflaged fatigues were digging in. It was my last day in the field. My scheduled rotation date back to the States was three days away. There was something familiar about this place.

I plotted the coordinates of our LZ on the map. We were several kilometers south of the Song Be River. A trail led off the LZ to the northeast. I traced the trail on the map with my index finger. There it was, less than a kilometer away from our LZ; it was marked as a "military area." It was the site of FSB Nashua, where I had taken command of Charlie Company on 1 January 1968.

I had volunteered to return to Vietnam during the summer of 1970, specifically requesting an advisory assignment with the South Vietnamese Army. American forces were withdrawing, and the Vietnamese badly needed advisory support. I was assigned as a senior advisor to the 44th Vietnamese Ranger Battalion in the Mekong Delta. When battalion-level advisory teams were phased out in IV Corps in May 1971, I became an advisor to a Vietnamese airborne battalion in III Corps. By then, U.S. participation in the war was all but over.

The significance of my final day of combat in Vietnam was not lost on me. The Warriors, who swept the battered jungles around me, were long gone. It was no longer their war. Only the ghosts of the fallen remained. Yet, the same determined enemy continued to hold this ground. They were prepared to fight on forever. For me, the war had come full circle. It was time to go home. Our nation would heal itself in time. Meanwhile, there was an Army to rebuild.

glossary

ACAV	An armored cavalry assault vehicle: a modified M113 armored personnel carrier
ACR	Armored Cavalry Regiment
AFN	Armed Forces Network
AK-47	A shoulder-fired Russian- or Chinese-manufactured assault rifle, standard weapon carried by Vietcong and North Vietnamese soldiers
AO	area of operations
APC	armored personnel carrier
ARA	aerial rocket artillery
Article 15	Nonjudicial punishment under the Uniform Code of Military Justice for violations of military law not warranting a court-martial
ARVN	Army of the Republic of (South) Vietnam
BMB	brigade main base
C4	Plastic explosive used for demolition tasks
C&C ship	command and control helicopter
CAR15	The carbine version of the M16 rifle, normally carried by lieutenants and captains in rifle companies

CAS	close air support
CG	commanding general
Chi-Com	Chinese Communist
Chinook	The CH-47 heavy-lift helicopter used by Army aviation
CIB	Combat Infantry Badge
Claymore	A U.S. antipersonnel mine
click	Slang for one kilometer
CMD	Capital Military District (Saigon)
CO	commanding officer
Cobra	AH-1 helicopter gunship
cold LZ	A helicopter landing zone having no enemy opposition
commo	communications
concertina	Coils of barbed wire used in defensive positions
Conex	A steel shipping container
COSVN	Central Office for South Vietnam: the central command for North Vietnam's operations in South Vietnam
CP	command post
C rations	combat field rations
Dai-uy	Vietnamese word for *captain*
DEFCON	A defensive concentration of artillery or mortar fire
DFC	Distinguished Flying Cross
DIVARTY	division artillery
DSC	Distinguished Service Cross
Duster	The M42 combat vehicle with twin 40mm cannons: originally designed for air defense, used primarily for ground defense in Vietnam
dust-off	Medical evacuation by helicopter: medevac
FAC	forward air controller

frag	fragmentation grenade
FO	forward observer (for artillery)
FSB	fire support base
grunt	infantryman
gunship	An armed helicopter that provides fire support for ground forces
H&I	harassment and interdiction (artillery fire)
hooch	Vietnamese hut
hot LZ	A helicopter landing zone opposed by enemy troops
Huey	UH-1 helicopter
I&R	intelligence and reconnaissance
KIA	killed in action
LAW	The M72 light antitank weapon, fired from the shoulder
LP	listening post
LRRP	long range reconnaissance patrol
LZ	landing zone (for helicopters)
M1	U.S. .30-caliber rifle used in WWII and Korea
M16	U.S. 5.56mm rifle used in Vietnam
M60	U.S. 7.62mm light machine gun used in Vietnam
M79	U.S. 40mm grenade launcher
MIA	missing in action
military crest	The area on the forward slope of a hill or ridge from which maximum observation covering the slope down to the base can be obtained
MOS	military occupational specialty
MP	military police
NCO	noncommissioned officer or sergeant
NDP	night defensive position
NVA	North Vietnamese Army

OCS	Officer Candidate School
PF	Popular Forces (South Vietnamese local militia forces)
POW	prisoner of war
PSP	pierced steel planking: used for makeshift runways and helipads
PX	post exchange
R&R	Rest and recreation, a five-day leave granted U.S. soldiers and usually taken out-of-country
Redcatchers	The nickname of the 199th Light Infantry Brigade
RF	Regional Forces (South Vietnamese)
ROTC	Reserve Officers Training Corps
RPG	Soviet- or Chinese-made rocket-propelled grenade with a shaped charge, a standard VC and NVA antiarmor weapon
RTO	radio telephone operator
S-1	staff personnel officer
S-2	staff intelligence officer
S-3	staff operations officer
S-3 Air	The staff operations officer responsible for planning and coordinating airmobile and air support of a battalion's operations
S-4	staff logistics officer
sapper	A VC or NVA soldier specially trained in infiltration and demolitions
short	Refers to the time remaining before an individual's tour of duty ends
SITREP	situation report
slick	The UH-1 troop-carrying or supply helicopter, also called Huey
Spooky	U.S. Air Force fixed-wing gunship, either AC-47 or AC-130

Starlight Scope	An optical night-vision scope
TAC	Tactical Air Command of U.S. Air Force, which provided fixed-wing tactical air support (known as *TAC air*) to ground forces
TF	task force
TOC	tactical operations center
Top	Slang for First Sergeant
track	An armored personnel carrier or armored cavalry vehicle
UCMJ	Uniform Code of Military Justice
VC	Vietcong
VNAF	Vietnamese Air Force (South)
WIA	wounded in action
WP	white phosphorus ammunition
XO	executive officer